VISUAL™
Quick Tips
Knitting

Visual®

by Sharon Turner

BICENTENNIAL
1807
WILEY
2007
BICENTENNIAL

Wiley Publishing, Inc.

Praise for the VISUAL Series

I just had to let you and your company know how great I think your books are. I just purchased my third Visual book (my first two are dog-eared now!) and, once again, your product has surpassed my expectations. The expertise, thought, and effort that go into each book are obvious, and I sincerely appreciate your efforts. Keep up the wonderful work!

—Tracey Moore (Memphis, TN)

I have several books from the Visual series and have always found them to be valuable resources.

—Stephen P. Miller (Ballston Spa, NY)

Thank you for the wonderful books you produce. It wasn't until I was an adult that I discovered how I learn—visually. Although a few publishers out there claim to present the material visually, nothing compares to Visual books. I love the simple layout. Everything is easy to follow. And I understand the material! You really know the way I think and learn. Thanks so much!

—Stacey Han (Avondale, AZ)

Like a lot of other people, I understand things best when I see them visually. Your books really make learning easy and life more fun.

—John T. Frey (Cadillac, MI)

I am an avid fan of your Visual books. If I need to learn anything, I just buy one of your books and learn the topic in no time. Wonders! I have even trained my friends to give me Visual books as gifts.

—Illona Bergstrom (Aventura, FL)

I write to extend my thanks and appreciation for your books. They are clear, easy to follow, and straight to the point. Keep up the good work! I bought several of your books and they are just right! No regrets! I will always buy your books because they are the best.

—Seward Kollie (Dakar, Senegal)

Credits

Acquisitions Editor
Pam Mourouzis

Project Editor
Donna Wright

Copy Editor
Marylouise Wiack

Editorial Manager
Christina Stambaugh

Publisher
Cindy Kitchel

Vice President and Executive Publisher
Kathy Nebenhaus

Interior Design
Kathie Rickard
Elizabeth Brooks

Cover Design
José Almaguer

Photography
Matt Bowen

About the Author

Sharon Turner designs knitwear and publishes a line of knitting patterns under the Trademark Monkeysuits. She is the author of *Monkeysuits: Sweaters and More to Knit for Kids*, *Teach Yourself Visually Knitting*, and *Teach Yourself Visually Knitting Design*. She lives in Brooklyn New York, with her husband and three daughters.

Acknowledgments

Thank you forever to my dear family. It's always a pleasure to work with Pam Mourouzis and Cindy Kitchel. Thanks also to Donna Wright, Marylouise Wiack, Shannon Ramsey, and Sherry Massey for all of their work on the book. Heartfelt appreciation goes to Ann Cannon-Brown, of elann.com, and Kirstin Muench, of Muench Yarns, who both very graciously supplied the beautiful yarns used for the how-to steps and swatches.

Instructional Videos Online

We've filmed videos of a few of the techniques described in this book—just look for the symbol. To view the videos, go to www.wiley.com/go/knittingvqt.

Table of Contents

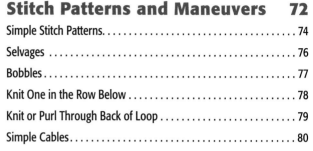

Stitch Patterns and Maneuvers 72

Knitting in the Round 82

Finishing Techniques 142

Finishing Details 162

Decorative Details 186

Appendix:
Reference Materials 206

Index 224

chapter 1

Knitting Necessities

Like any hobby, knitting requires unique materials and tools: yarn, knitting needles, and other gear to make knitting easier. You can use this chapter to learn about yarn properties and types, and the meaning of all of that small print on the yarn label. Knitting needles come in many shapes and sizes, so choosing which type to use can be confusing. These pages explain needle types, sizes, and materials, as well as what each is used for. This chapter also includes a summary of knitting extras—such as stitch holders, ring markers, and needle gauges—and what purpose they serve.

Knitting Needles

Knitting needles come in many shapes, sizes, and materials. Certain projects benefit from particular needles. For example, you may want to use wood or bamboo when knitting lace so that loose stitches don't slide off easily.

TYPES OF NEEDLES

Knitting needles come in metal, plastic, wood, and bamboo, and each needle type offers certain advantages. For example, yarn slides easily along metal, and plastic needles are lightweight but can bend. Wood needles are beautiful, although they can be more expensive than metal or plastic. Bamboo needles are lighter and less expensive than wood. Some beginners prefer bamboo because the surface slows yarn from slipping off the needle.

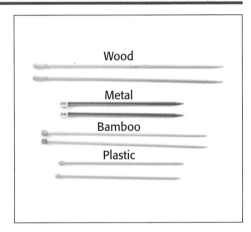

SHAPES OF NEEDLES

Straight, or single-point, needles come in various lengths and have a point on one end and a knob on the other. They are good for flat knitting.

Double-pointed needles are pointed on both ends and are sold in sets of four or five. They're good for small projects that are knit in the round.

Circular needles, which have two points connected by a nylon cord, come in a variety of lengths and materials. They're good for knitting large projects in the round. You can also use them for large flat knitting, as well as long edgings on garments.

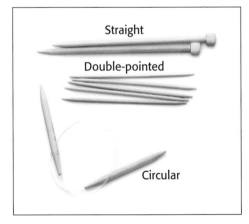

SIZES OF NEEDLES

Needle sizing can be confusing because each needle has three numbers that indicate the size. The most important number is the diameter of the needle shaft, which is measured in millimeters (mm). In general, small-diameter needles are used for thin yarns, and large-diameter needles are used for thick yarns.

The second number, representing the U.S. numbering system, labels sizes ranging from 0, for the thinnest needle, to 50 for the thickest needle. The third number on a needle is the length of the needle's shaft. This number is generally represented on the needle package in both inches and centimeters.

The chart below shows needle sizes in metric as well as the corresponding U.S. numbering.

Needle Sizes							
Metric (mm)	**U.S.**		**Metric (mm)**	**U.S.**		**Metric (mm)**	**U.S.**
2.0	0		4.5	7		9.0	13
2.25–2.5	1		5.0	8		10.0	15
2.75	2		5.5	9		12.0–12.75	17
3.0	–		6.0	10		16.0	19
3.25	3		6.5	10½		19.0	35
3.5	4		7.0	10¾		20.0	36
3.75	5		7.5	–		25.0	50
4.0	6		8.0	11			

POINTS OF NEEDLES

Some knitting needles have a dull, rounded tip, some have a long, tapering point, and some even have a concave shape to the point. Certain points are better suited to specific jobs. For example, when working bobbles, where you knit many times into the same stitch, the knitting can become so tight that it's difficult to insert a more rounded needle tip. You need to use a pointier tip for this and other firm knitting. A concave point works well for lace, cables, and other patterns that require frequent stitch handling and moving. A rounded point is good for loose, relaxed knitting.

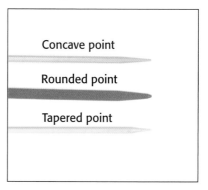

Concave point

Rounded point

Tapered point

Knitting Accessories

In addition to needles and yarn, you need to equip yourself with some knitting accessories.

YOUR KNITTING BAG

Choose a knitting bag that stands open and has a smooth interior and a lot of pockets for accessories. Watch out for Velcro fasteners—your yarn can become snagged and damaged on them. Look for big knitting bags for home and car travel, and small-project drawstring bags that you can take on short outings.

ESSENTIAL ACCESSORIES

Equip yourself with a small pair of scissors and a tape measure. You can find folding scissors at fabric or yarn stores—these won't poke through your bag or into your knitting. Retractable tape measures are nice and neat, too. You also need tapestry needles, or yarn needles, for sewing knit pieces together and darning in loose ends. A stitch-and-needle gauge is a handy all-in-one tool: You can use it to measure your stitch-and-row gauge and knitting needle diameter. Point protectors will help to hold your knitting on the needle when you store it away. A row counter that attaches to the needle will help you keep track of where you are in a pattern.

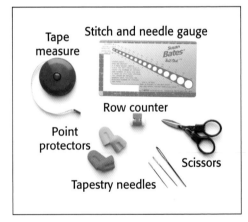

Tape measure

Stitch and needle gauge

Row counter

Point protectors

Tapestry needles

Scissors

OTHER ACCESSORIES

It's not a bad idea to carry a stitch holder or two, stitch markers, plastic-headed straight pins, and a cable needle in your bag, but it's not absolutely necessary. As an alternative, you can substitute scrap yarn for stitch markers and holders.

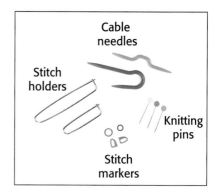

Cable needles

Stitch holders

Knitting pins

Stitch markers

HANDY EXTRAS

Pompom makers are great for forming perfectly round, tight pompoms. Crochet hooks come in handy for making edgings and ties, and in some cases for special bind-offs. Plastic bobbins help you to organize your colors for intarsia knitting.

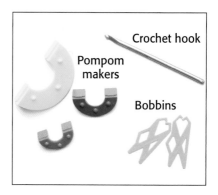

Crochet hook

Pompom makers

Bobbins

TIP

A Safer Way to Carry Scissors

If you don't have the little scissors that fold, you might accidentally cut your knitting if you store your scissors with your project. You can slip a knitting needle point protector onto the sharp end of your scissors to protect your yarn and projects.

Knitting yarns come in many fibers, weights, and textures. Below is a general guide covering the most common yarn types.

NATURAL FIBERS

Natural fibers come from animals and plants. Yarns spun from animal fibers, like wool, alpaca, mohair, cashmere, and angora, are generally the warmest to wear and hold their shape well. Wool comes in a range of textures, from sometimes-scratchy Shetlands, to softer merinos. Alpaca is a luxuriously soft fiber that has a lot of drape. Mohair is hairier than wool, and mohair-only garments have a fuzzy halo. Cashmere comes from goats and is the softest and most expensive fiber. Angora, which comes from rabbits, is also extremely soft and fuzzy. Silk, the fiber produced by silkworms, is warm but not as elastic as wool. Garments made from cotton and linen yarns are generally good for warm-weather wear, but they are heavier and less elastic than wool.

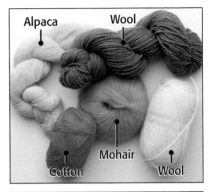
Alpaca Wool Mohair Cotton Wool

SYNTHETIC FIBERS

Synthetics include acrylic, nylon, and polyester. These yarns are human-made and are often less expensive than natural fibers. Many are machine washable.

Acrylic Nylon Polyester

TIP

Wind a Center-Pull Ball

You don't need a mechanical ball winder to wind your own center-pull skein. You can start with an old spool, a short, thick dowel, or even a small piece of rolled-up paper. Keeping a 5 or 6-inch tail sticking up from the top of the spool or the dowel, begin winding—loosely, so as not to stretch all of the spring out of your yarn. When you're done winding, tuck the outside end under some of the wrapped yarn strands, and begin knitting with the end coming up out of the center.

BLENDS

Two or more fibers can be combined and spun into one yarn, creating a blend. Some fibers are blended to produce less expensive or easier-care yarns. Another benefit of blending is that mixing one fiber with another can alter certain characteristics of that fiber. For example, cotton can be improved in body and elasticity by being combined with acrylic; combining wool with alpaca, angora, or cashmere softens it.

Wool/llama
Cotton/acrylic
Cotton/alpaca
Wool/acrylic
Wool/alpaca/cashmere

NOVELTY YARNS

Furry, metallic, and bumpy yarns are called *novelty yarns*. These yarns work well for trims and dressy garments, and they can be doubled with another yarn for added texture and color. It is often difficult to see stitches clearly in a fabric knit in highly textured novelty yarns; as a result, if you are working something like seed stitch, intricate cables, lace patterns, or detailed color work, you will probably want to choose something with better stitch definition.

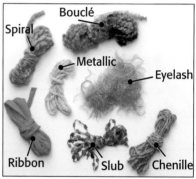

Bouclé
Spiral
Metallic
Eyelash
Ribbon
Slub
Chenille

YARN WEIGHTS

Yarn comes in many thicknesses and is labeled—from thinnest to thickest—as super-fine, fine, light, medium, bulky, and super-bulky. Super-fine yarns include fingering, baby, lace-weight, and many sock yarns. Fine yarns generally encompass sport weight and some baby yarns. Light yarns include double-knitting, and light worsted. Medium yarns are also called worsted, aran, or afghan yarn. Bulky refers to yarns that are labeled as chunky or heavy worsted. Super-bulky yarns are sometimes called polar or roving. Fine yarns require thin needles, while bulky yarns require thick needles.

| Super-fine |
| Fine |
| Light |
| Medium |
| Bulky |
| Super-bulky |

Understanding Yarn Labels

Most commercially produced yarns come with a label, or ball band. Always save the ball band with the yarn; it contains useful information.

The largest print on the ball band is the yarn manufacturer's name and logo, and then the name of that particular yarn. The ball band also includes the fiber content of the yarn.

The ball band lists the weight of the ball and the *yardage*, or the length of yarn contained in the ball. Yarn companies assign numbers to indicate yarn color. These numbers differ from one manufacturer to the next. Also listed is a dye lot number. Yarns are dyed in large batches, or lots; the dye lot number refers to a particular batch of a color. It's important to buy enough yarn from the same dye lot for a project because color differs from one dye lot to the next.

The ball band also lists what size knitting needles to use with the yarn, and what the desired gauge is for that yarn when it is knit with those needles.

TIP

Substitute Yarn by Yardage, Not by Weight

Using the term *weight* when describing yarn can be confusing, as it can refer to how much a particular ball of yarn weighs, regardless of the yarn's thickness. When substituting yarns according to a pattern's specifications, be sure to buy the same yarn weight—in this case, thickness—by the same *yardage*, not by how much the ball weighs. For example, if the pattern specifies 10 balls of yarn that is 100 yards per 50-gram ball, then you would buy 1,000 yards of the substitute yarn, assuming that it knits to the same gauge—not 500 grams of substitute yarn. The yardage of a 50-gram ball can vary greatly between yarns of similar gauge. It all depends on fiber content and how densely the yarn is spun.

Weight 100g/220 yards

Needle size:
7 = 5 st per 1î
8 = 4½ st per 1″

Col. no. 32
Lot no. 1077

fine wool yarns
Soft & Thick

Made in the U.S.A.

90% Merino Wool
5% Alpaca
5% Cashmere

Care Instructions and Symbols

You should become familiar with the symbols that are used to indicate care instructions for particular yarns. You need to know this information when it comes time to clean your hand-knit items.

Symbols using the image of a washing machine or tub indicate whether a fiber is machine- or hand-washable. The symbol of the tub with an X over it means that the fiber is neither machine- nor hand-washable. The triangular symbols indicate bleaching instructions.

Symbols using the image of an iron indicate whether a fiber can be pressed. The symbol of the iron with dots in it illustrates what temperature should be used when pressing.

Circular symbols illustrate dry-cleaning instructions. If the circle has an X through it, the fiber should not be dry-cleaned. Circles with letters in them indicate which chemicals should be used to dry-clean the fiber. Your dry-cleaner should be able to tell you what solvents they use.

TIP

Softening Scratchy Knits

Although fun to knit with, some wools are scratchy to wear or irritable to sensitive skin. You can soften rough knits by hand-washing them in a small amount of cool water mixed with a few teaspoons of hair conditioner. Just as it smoothes your hair, plain white hair conditioner can work wonders on wool.

MACHINE WASH TEMPERATURE	**BLEACH**	**IRON** TEMPERATURE (Dry or Steam)	**DRY-CLEAN** TEMPERATURE
Do Not Wash	Do Not Bleach	Do Not Iron	Do Not Dry-Clean
Hand Wash	Any Bleach (when needed)	Low	(F) Dry-Clean, Petroleum Solvent Only
Normal		Medium	(P) Dry-Clean, Any Solvent Except Trichloroethylene
 Delicate/Gentle		High	(A) Dry-Clean, Any Solvent
Cool/Cold			
Warm			
Hot			

Casting On

Before you begin knitting, you need to cast on, or put a foundation row of stitches onto your needles. There are several cast-on techniques, all serving different purposes and achieving varied results. This chapter covers five methods that should carry you through most situations.

The first stitch that you cast on to your needle is a slipknot. Here's an easy way to make one.

① Starting about 10 inches in from the end of your yarn, make a loop.

② Pull the working yarn behind the loop as shown. Insert the needle underneath the working yarn and pull it up through the loop.

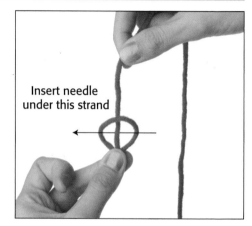

Insert needle
under this strand

③ Pull the ends of the yarn so that the slipknot sits snugly on the needle.

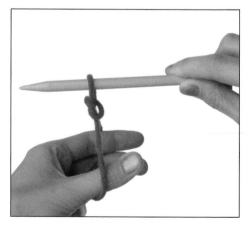

This quick-and-easy cast-on is handy for casting on stitches mid-row for buttonholes and pockets. However, as a foundation row, it does not produce the neatest edge; you should use one of the other methods as a foundation row for fine knits.

1 Have your needle ready with a slip-knot on it. Holding the needle in your right hand and the working yarn in your left, make a loop with the working yarn.

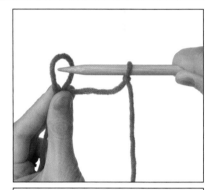

2 Place the loop on the needle with your left hand and then pull the working yarn to tighten.

3 Repeat steps 1–2 until you have the desired number of stitches on the needle.

TIP

A Neater First Row

It's hard to knit a neat first row with the simple cast-on. Because the cast-on loops aren't knotted onto the needle, you get an increasingly long strand of yarn between the stitches as you knit the row. You can alleviate this somewhat by pulling the stitches up and enlarging them slightly as you knit across. Simply insert the right needle into the cast-on loop, pull the right needle up a bit to make the stitch larger, and then knit it as usual. Continue this across the row, without pulling the needles apart between stitches, and you'll have a fairly neat first row.

The knit cast-on produces an elegant elastic edge. You start with a slipknot on your left needle and then use the right needle to work the stitch as if you are going to knit it; however, instead of taking it off the needle, you place the new stitch back onto the left needle.

---

1 Have your needle ready with a slipknot on it. Holding this needle in your left hand and an empty needle in your right hand, insert the right needle into the stitch from front to back, as if to knit.

2 Wrap the working yarn around the tip of the right needle and pull up a loop, as when knitting a stitch.

3 Keeping the stitch on the needle, use the right needle to place the pulled-up loop on the left needle.

4 Pull the working yarn to tighten.

5 Repeat steps 1–4, placing each new stitch above the previously cast-on stitch until you have the desired number of stitches on the left needle.

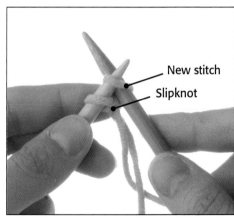

New stitch

Slipknot

Cable Cast-On

The cable cast-on is performed like the knit cast-on, except the needle is inserted between two stitches before the loop is pulled up. It produces an attractive, ropelike edge on both sides of the knitting. However, it is not as elastic as the knit cast-on, and so it is good for buttonholes and non-ribbed edgings. You should use a different cast-on if you require a flexible edge.

① Perform steps 1–4 of the knit cast-on. You should have 2 stitches on your needle—the slipknot and 1 new stitch.

② Insert the right needle between the 2 stitches, and not into their loops. Wrap the working yarn around the tip of the right needle and pull up a loop, as you would when knitting a stitch.

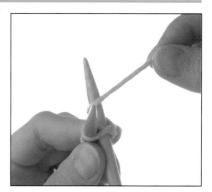

③ Leaving the 2 initial stitches on the needle, use the right needle to place the pulled-up loop on the left needle.

④ Repeat steps 2–3, placing each new stitch above the previously cast-on stitch until you have the desired number of stitches on the left needle.

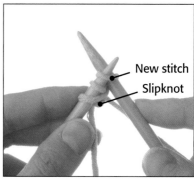

New stitch

Slipknot

TIP

A Very Elastic Edge
Even highly elastic cast-ons can be too tight for some projects, like sock or mitten cuffs. When casting on for something that requires a very resilient edge, try this: Cast onto needles a size or two larger than the size that you should use for the project; then, when you begin knitting, switch to the correct size.

Long-Tail Cast-On

The long-tail cast-on, or slingshot cast-on, looks complicated at first, but once you master it, it's easy and fast. It produces a neat, elastic edge that looks ropelike on one side and like a row of bumps on the other. You can choose which edge to show on the right side. To make the ropelike edge appear on the right side, you must work your first row after casting on as a wrong-side row.

1 Put a slipknot on your needle, leaving a tail that is the equivalent of 1 inch for each stitch that you plan to cast on, plus a few more inches. For example, if you plan to cast on 12 stitches, leave a tail that is about 15 inches long.

2 Hold the yarn with the tail wrapped over your thumb, and the working yarn over your forefinger, grasping both ends with your pinky and ring finger in the center of your palm.

3 Lower the needle to create a V while holding the slipknot in place with your right forefinger.

4 Insert the needle up and under the yarn that is looped around the outside of your thumb.

5 Move the needle to the right, and use it to grab the yarn from the nearest side of your forefinger.

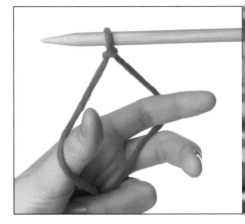

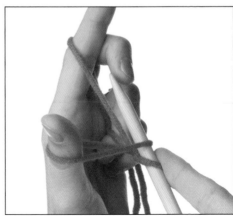

6 Pull it through the loop between your thumb and the needle.

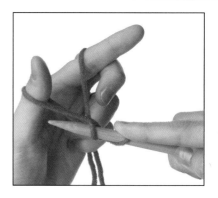

7 Drop the loops from your thumb and fore-finger, and pull both ends of the yarn to tighten the stitch on the needle.

You have just cast on 1 stitch.

8 Repeat steps 2–7 until you have cast on the desired number of stitches.

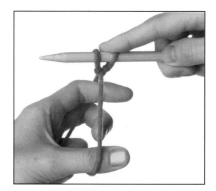

TIP

Is your yarn losing its twist?

Casting on stitches using the long-tail method often causes the tail yarn to lose some of its twist. It ends up looking looser and messier the farther you go. The tail is the yarn wrapped around your thumb, and every time you insert the needle and then drop that loop, you're turning it inside out, causing the tail to untwist a little. You can give a little twist back by pausing every now and then to drop the tail, allowing it to re-twist. As you get toward the end, you can manually twirl the tail a little to finish up neatly.

You use the open, or provisional, cast-on when you want to be able to access the cast-on edge as "live" stitches to be worked later. For example, you might want to work a lacy border or add a peplum or hem to your lower edge. This open method is worked very much like the long-tail cast-on, only you need a length of scrap yarn—something strong yet slippery, like mercerized cotton.

1 Pull out a strand from your working yarn that is the equivalent of ½ inch per stitch that you plan to cast on, plus a few more inches, leaving it attached to the ball. For example, if you plan to cast on 30 stitches, pull a strand that is about 18 inches long. Cut a strand of waste yarn the same length and knot the two strands together so that the ends line up.

2 Holding the yarns and a needle in your right hand, hold the knot against the needle with your thumb.

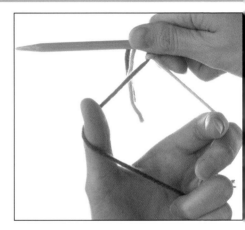

3 Take the yarns in your left hand, holding them as you would for the long-tail method, with the working yarn around your thumb and the waste yarn over your forefinger, grasping both ends with your pinky and ring finger in the center of your palm.

4 Work as you would with the long-tail method, inserting the needle up and under the working yarn that is looped around the outside of your thumb; then move the needle to the right and use it to grab the waste yarn from the nearest side of your forefinger.

5 Pull the waste yarn through the loop between your thumb and the needle.

6 Drop the loops from your thumb and forefinger and pull both ends of the yarn to tighten the stitch on the needle.

You have just cast on 1 stitch.

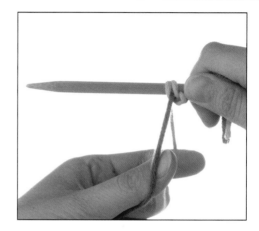

7 Repeat steps 4–6 until you have cast on the desired number of stitches.

8 When you need the stitches to be "live" again, carefully snip the waste yarn from each stitch, slipping the freed stitches onto a needle as you go.

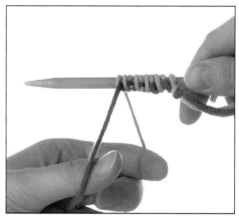

Knitting, Purling, and Slipping Stitches

A knit fabric is made up of rows and rows of loops formed by knit stitches and/or purl stitches. Some knitters use their right hand to work the yarn; this is called the English method. Others work the yarn with their left hand—the Continental method. Instructions for both methods are covered here, along with a couple of extras—slipping stitches and joining new yarn.

Many Americans use the English method—holding the yarn with the right hand—but you don't have to be right-handed to use this method.

1 Hold the needle with the cast-on stitches on it in your left hand and the empty needle in your right hand, with the working yarn wound around the fingers of your right hand.

2 Holding the yarn in back of both needles, insert the right needle into the front of the first stitch on the left needle.

Your needles will form an X, with the right needle behind the left needle.

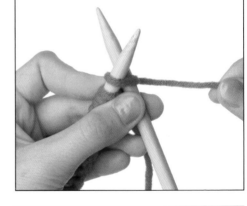

3 Holding the crossed needles between your left thumb and forefinger, bring the working yarn around the right needle from back to front and then down between the 2 needles.

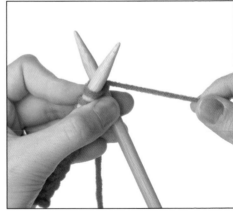

4 Pull the right needle toward the front, bringing the new loop of yarn that you just wrapped around it through the cast-on stitch, and slip the cast-on stitch off the left needle.

You now have 1 stitch on the right needle.

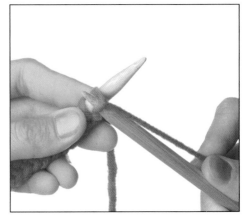

5 Repeat steps 2–4 for each remaining cast-on stitch until all of the new stitches are on the right needle.

You have now completed 1 row of knitting.

6 Switch the needle with the stitches on it to your left hand and repeat steps 2–5 for each row.

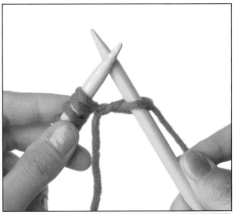

TIP

Is your knitting too tight?

If you find that your knitting is so tight that it is difficult to slide your stitches along the needle, you are probably doing one of the following three things. First, you may be inserting the right needle only partway through the stitch—thereby producing smaller stitches on the narrower, pointed end of the needle. This is like using a smaller needle to knit. Be sure to push the right needle to its full diameter through each new stitch.

Knit: Continental Method

To knit using the Continental method, you hold the yarn and control the tension with your left hand. Don't worry if you are right-handed, though: Both right-handed and left-handed knitters have been knitting this way for centuries.

Most knitters who use this method find it faster than the English method, as the yarn is wrapped around the needle with a simple flick of the finger.

---

① Hold the needle with the cast-on stitches on it in your left hand and the empty needle in your right hand, with the working yarn wound around the fingers of your left hand.

② Insert the right needle into the front of the first stitch on the left needle, holding the yarn in back of both needles.

Your needles will form an X, with the right needle behind the left needle.

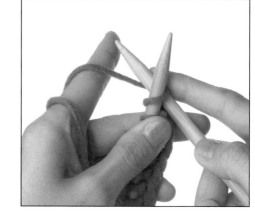

③ Use your left forefinger to wrap the yarn around the right needle from front to back.

Note: *This small, quick motion primarily involves the left forefinger. You can help it along by grabbing the yarn with the right needle at the same time.*

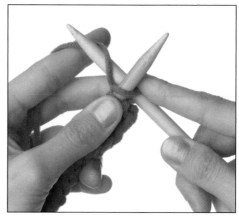

4 Pull the right needle toward the front, bringing the new loop of yarn that you just wrapped around it through the cast-on stitch, and slip the cast-on stitch off the left needle.

You now have 1 stitch on the right needle.

Note: You may want to use your right forefinger to keep the wrapped strand from slipping off the tip of the needle.

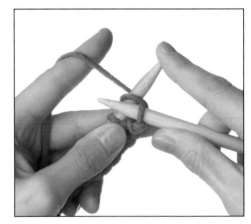

5 Repeat steps 2–4 for each remaining cast-on stitch until all of the new stitches are on the right needle.

You have now completed 1 row of knitting.

6 Switch the needle with the stitches on it to your left hand and repeat steps 2–5 for each row.

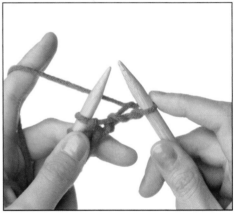

TIP

More Fixes for Too-Tight Knitting

You may be tugging on the working yarn a little too sharply after knitting each stitch. This unnecessary action makes your knitting too tight and also slows you down and interrupts the relaxing rhythm of knitting. Another factor in knitting too tightly is winding the working yarn so snugly around your fingers and hand that it doesn't slide easily from the ball through your fingers and into your knitting. You need to try a new way of guiding the yarn through your fingers.

Purling is the opposite of knitting. You hold the needles the same way as for knitting English style, but you keep the yarn in front of the needles instead of at the back.

① Hold the needle with the cast-on stitches on it in your left hand, and hold both the empty needle and the working yarn in your right hand.

② Holding the yarn in front of both needles, insert the right needle from back to front (that is, from right to left) into the first stitch on the left needle.

Your needles will form an X, with the right needle in front of the left needle.

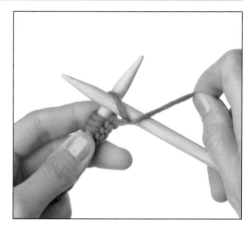

③ Hold the crossed needles between your left thumb and forefinger and bring the yarn behind the right needle, or between the crossed needles; then wrap the yarn around the right needle counter-clockwise.

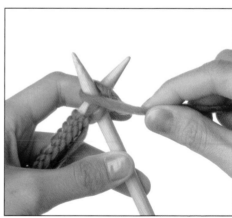

④ Pull the right needle toward the back, bringing the new loop of yarn that you just wrapped around it through the cast-on stitch; then slip the cast-on stitch off the left needle.

You now have 1 stitch on the right needle.

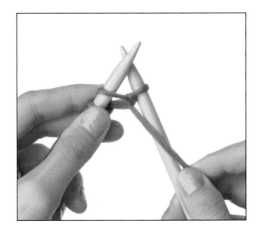

⑤ Repeat steps 2–4 for each remaining cast-on stitch until all of the new stitches are on the right needle.

You have now completed 1 row of purling.

⑥ Switch the needle with stitches on it back to your left hand and repeat steps 2–5 for each row.

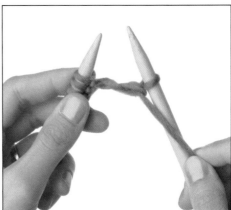

TIP

Recognizing Knit Stitches and Purl Stitches

Sometimes beginners have trouble figuring out which is the knit side and which is the purl side when working in stockinette stitch (knitting the right-side rows and purling the wrong-side rows). The smooth side that is made up of columns of V's is the knit side; the bumpy side made up of ladders is the purl side.

Purl: Continental Method

When you purl using the Continental method, you not only hold the yarn and control tension with your left hand, but you also hold the yarn in front of the needles, as for the English method.

The Continental method makes it easier to move the yarn from the front of the needles to the back of the needles in the same row. As a result, when you work ribbing or seed stitch using the Continental method, you really feel the difference.

① Hold the needle with the cast-on stitches on it in your left hand, and hold both the empty needle and the working yarn wound around the fingers of your left hand.

② Holding the yarn in front of both needles, insert the right needle from back to front (that is, from right to left) into the first stitch on the left needle.

Your needles will form an X, with the right needle in front of the left needle.

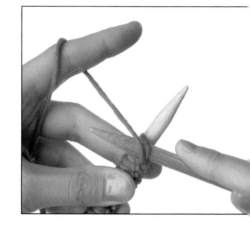

③ Use your left forefinger to wrap the yarn around the right needle from front to back, between the needles, and back to the front of the right needle.

Note: This is a small, quick motion that involves flicking your left forefinger down, bringing the yarn between the needles and then back up, and creating a loop on the right needle.

4 Pull the right needle toward the back, bringing the new loop of yarn that you just wrapped around it through the cast-on stitch (a); then slip the cast-on stitch off the left needle (b).

You now have 1 stitch on the right needle.

Note: You may want to use your right forefinger to keep the wrapped strand from slipping off the tip of the needle at step 4a.

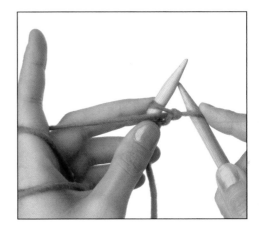

5 Repeat steps 2–4 for each remaining cast-on stitch, until all of the new stitches are on the right needle.

You have now completed 1 row of purling.

6 Switch the needle with stitches on it back to your left hand and repeat steps 2–5 for each row.

TIP

Getting uneven tension with the continental method?

Some knitters find that their stockinette stitch looks uneven when they knit Continental style. For some reason, the purl rows are looser, and look slightly raised on the knit side. If you are having the same problem, you can use a needle one size smaller for all of the purl rows to compensate.

When knitting instructions tell you to slip a stitch, it usually means you move the stitch from the left needle to the right needle, without knitting or purling it. Slipped stitches are often used for decreases and textured stitch patterns, heel flaps, and edge stitches.

SLIP A STITCH KNITWISE

1. Insert the right needle from front to back (knitwise) into the next stitch on the left needle.

2. Without knitting the stitch, slip it from the left needle to the right needle.

SLIP A STITCH PURLWISE

1. Insert the right needle from back to front (purlwise) into the next stitch on the left needle.

2. Without purling the stitch, slip it from the left needle onto the right needle.

TIP

Should I slip knitwise or purlwise?

Usually knitting instructions will state whether to slip a stitch as if to knit (knitwise), or as if to purl (purlwise). If the instructions don't say, then you should probably slip the stitch purlwise. Slipping the stitch purlwise simply moves it from the left needle to the right, while slipping a stitch knitwise moves it from the left needle to the right *and* twists the stitch at the same time.

When your first ball of yarn has length remaining that is less than four times the width of your knitting, or if you're working stripes and it is time for a new color, then it's time to join new yarn. It's better to join a new ball at the beginning of a row than in the middle. That way, you can sew your loose ends into a seam or an edge.

1 Finish your row and cut off the old yarn, leaving a 6-inch tail.

2 Tie a 6-inch end from your new ball snugly onto the tail of the old yarn.

3 Taking care not to confuse the new working yarn with the tied end, work across the row as usual.

Note: When you finish your project, you can untie the knot and weave in the ends to hide them.

TIP

Sewing Seams with Yarn Ends

If you like to backstitch your seams, you can use the yarn ends that accumulate from casting on and joining new yarn to sew them. If that is your plan, leave tails that are longer than 6 inches when casting on and joining new yarns so that you will have enough length to sew the seams. You save a lot of weaving in of ends this way.

chapter 4

Binding Off Stitches

Binding off is what you do when you want to get your stitches off the needle permanently, without allowing them to unravel. You may bind off at the very end of a project to finish it, or you may shape your garment's armholes or neck by binding off a few stitches here and there. You can also bind off in a decorative way to create an elegant edging on a finished piece.

Bind Off Knitwise

Binding off knitwise is the most frequently used and easiest bind-off. You use it to bind off knit stitches. Remember to keep it loose.

① Knit until you have a total of 2 stitches on the right needle; then insert the left needle into the front of the first stitch that you knitted onto the right needle.

② Pull the first stitch over the second knit stitch and off the right needle.

You have now bound off 1 stitch knitwise, and you have 1 stitch on the right needle.

③ Repeat steps 1–2 until you have bound off the desired number of stitches.

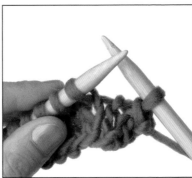

TIP

Binding Off Loosely

You often see the instruction "Bind off loosely" in knitting patterns. You bind off loosely so that your finished edge has elasticity, and so that the knitting retains its width. An easy way to ensure a loose but even bind-off is to use a needle that is one, two, or even three sizes larger than the needle used for the body of your garment.

This method is just like the knit bind-off, except that you purl instead of knit. You use it to bind off purl stitches.

1. Purl until you have 2 stitches on the right needle; then insert the left needle into the front of the first stitch that you purled onto the right needle.

2. Pull the first stitch over the second purled stitch and off the right needle.

   You have now bound off 1 stitch purlwise, and you have 1 stitch on the right needle.

3. Repeat steps 1–2 until you have bound off the desired number of stitches.

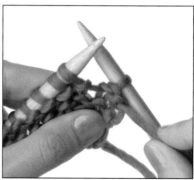

TIP

Binding Off the Last Stitch, and Some Tips for Doing It Neatly

When you have only 1 stitch remaining on the right needle, cut your working yarn, leaving a tail at least 6 inches long. Thread this tail through the last stitch and pull tight. If this leaves you with a big loop sticking off the edge, one solution is to slip the first stitch purlwise when you work the row *before* the bind-off row. Another solution is to knit this last stitch on the bind-off row with the corresponding stitch in the row below. Insert the right needle through the back of the stitch in the row below, slip it onto the left needle with the last stitch, and knit the two together.

You should always bind off in pattern, unless the instructions say otherwise. Binding off in pattern is simply working the stitch pattern and binding off at the same time. Your finished project will have a more refined look, and your ribbings will remain elastic. As an example, here is how to bind off in 1 × 1 rib.

1 Knit 1, purl 1.

You now have 2 stitches on the right needle.

2 Insert the left needle into the front of the first stitch (the knit stitch) on the right needle.

3 Pull the first stitch over the second stitch (the purl stitch) and off the right needle.

You have now bound off 1 stitch in pattern, and you have 1 purl stitch on the right needle.

4 Knit the next stitch on the left needle.

5 Insert the left needle into the front of the first stitch (the purl stitch) on the right needle.

6 Pull the first stitch over the second stitch (the knit stitch) and off the right needle.

You have now bound off 2 stitches in pattern, and you have 1 knit stitch on the right needle.

7 Continue working the rib pattern and binding off as you go.

TIP

Counting Bound-Off Stitches

It's easy to become confused when instructed to bind off a certain number of stitches at the beginning of a row, as you would for an armhole or neck shaping. You need 2 stitches on the right needle to bind off 1; remember to count the stitches that are actually pulled over and off the needle, not the number of stitches that are knit and/or purled.

Bind Off in Knitted Cord

Here's a nice finish to a bound-off edge. You can bind off in knitted cord, which creates a neat tubular border. This is great for brims on top-down hats, cuffs for toe-up socks, and edgings on bags, scarves, and blankets.

1. Use the simple cast-on (see p. 17) to cast on 3 additional stitches for the knitted cord to the beginning of your row.

   Now you're ready to begin the knitted cord bind-off.

2. Knit the first 2 stitches.

3. Slip the next stitch as if to knit.

4. Knit the next stitch.

   You now have 4 stitches on the right needle.

5. Insert the right needle into the slipped stitch through the front, and lift it over the knit stitch and off the right needle.

6. Slip the 3 stitches as if to purl, one at a time, back to the left needle.

7. Without turning work, pull the working yarn snugly across the back of the first 3 stitches. You are now ready to work the beginning of the row again.

8. Repeat steps 2–7 until all of the original stitches have been bound off, and only the 3 knitted cord stitches remain.

9. Cut the yarn, leaving a 6-inch tail; pull through the 3 knitted cord stitches and tighten.

Three-Needle Bind-Off

The three-needle bind-off is excellent for binding off and joining horizontal seams at the same time. Shoulders that have been shaped with short rows, or that have not been shaped at all, are perfect candidates for the three-needle bind-off. To work it, you must have the same number of stitches for each piece.

Put each set of stitches on knitting needles, and have a third knitting needle handy. If one of the sets of stitches has the working yarn still attached, you can use that yarn to perform the bind-off; otherwise, use a piece of the same yarn that you used to knit the pieces.

---

1. Hold the needles with the stitches on them parallel, with the right sides of your knitting facing each other.

2. Insert a third knitting needle into the first stitch on the front needle as if to knit, and then into the first stitch on the back needle as if to knit. Wrap the working yarn around the tip of the third needle as you would to knit normally.

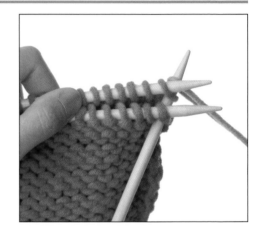

3. Bring the loop through the first stitch on the back needle, just as you would to knit, and then all the way through to the front of the first stitch on the front needle.

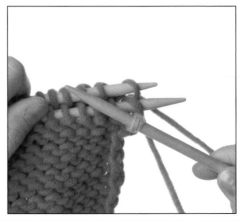

4. Slip both old stitches off the parallel needles, just as you would to knit them.

   You now have 1 stitch on the third needle.

5. Repeat steps 2–4. You should now have 2 stitches on the right needle.

6. Pass the first stitch on the right needle over the second stitch to bind off.

7. Continue knitting together the corresponding stitches from each needle and binding off as you go, until only 1 stitch remains on the right needle. Cut the yarn, leaving a 6-inch tail, and pull the tail through the last stitch to secure it.

8. Weave in the loose ends.

   Note: A contrast color yarn was used here to bind off the seam for illustrative purposes. Be sure to work your three-needle bind-off with the same yarn that you used to knit your pieces.

chapter 5

Correcting Mistakes

Has a mysterious hole appeared in your knitting? Do you have fewer stitches on your needle than you should? Dropped stitches, twisted stitches, incomplete stitches—these are all common errors that beginners (and even experts!) make. You can fix them easily by using the methods in this chapter.

Correct a Twisted Stitch

Sometimes stitches become twisted, resulting in an uneven finish to the knit fabric. To recognize the problem, you need to know how stitches should sit on the needle. When you look at the stitches on your needle, the right side of each loop should rest on the front of the needle, and the left side of each loop should rest against the back of the needle. If you see a stitch where the left side of the loop is in the front, then you have a twisted stitch.

① Work across until you get to the twisted stitch.

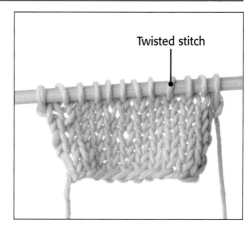

Twisted stitch

② Use the right needle to pick up the twisted stitch from the left needle, as shown, turn it around, and place it back on the left needle so that the right side of the loop is in front.

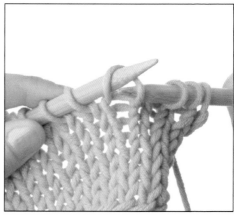

Correct an Incomplete Stitch

A stitch is incomplete when the working yarn is not pulled through the loop. The stitch is transferred from the left needle to the right needle, but it is not knit or purled; the working yarn is wrapped over the needle, crossing over the mistakenly slipped stitch.

---

1 Work across until you get to the incomplete stitch.

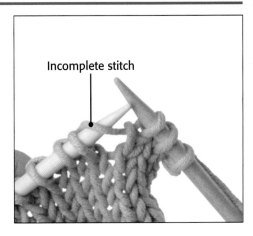

Incomplete stitch

2 Insert the right needle as if to purl (from back to front) into the incomplete stitch. Pull it over the unworked strand and off the needle.

Pick Up a Dropped Stitch One Row Below

A dropped stitch is a stitch that has slipped off your needles. If you find that you have dropped a stitch on the row before the row that you're currently working, you can fix it with your knitting needle using this method.

① Work across until you get to the dropped stitch.

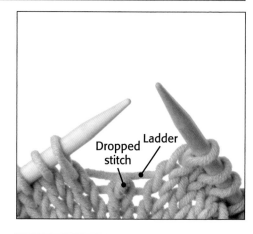

Dropped stitch

Ladder

② Insert the right needle into the dropped stitch and under the horizontal strand (the "ladder") behind the dropped stitch.

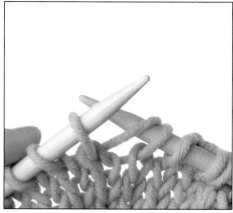

③ Insert the left needle from back to front into the dropped stitch on the right needle, and pull it over the ladder and off the right needle.

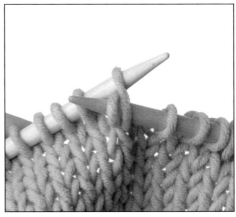

④ Use the right needle to transfer the repaired stitch back to the left needle.

The repaired stitch is ready to be worked as usual.

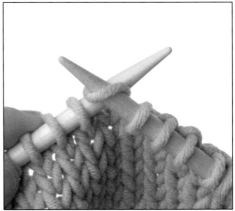

TIP

Picking Up a Dropped Stitch One Row Below on the Purl Side

If you drop a stitch and need to correct it when you're on a purl row, you can turn your work around and correct it as shown above. You can also work from the purl side; remember that front and back are reversed. As a result, you must insert the right needle into the dropped stitch as if to purl, and at step 4, you must insert the left needle into the back of the repaired stitch to transfer it back to the left needle.

Pick Up a Dropped Stitch Several Rows Below

A dropped stitch that has unraveled several or more rows is called a *run*. To repair a run, you can use a crochet hook that is the appropriate size for your yarn. If you're working on the purl side when you discover the run, you just turn your work to the knit side to correct it.

① Work across until you get to the dropped stitch.

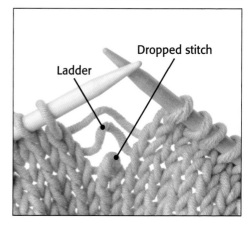

Dropped stitch

Ladder

② Insert the crochet hook from front to back into the dropped stitch. Pull the lowest horizontal ladder from back to front through the dropped stitch.

③ Repeat step 2 until you have no ladders left.

④ Place the repaired stitch onto the left needle, being sure not to twist it.

The repaired stitch is ready to be worked as usual.

TIP

Are there too many stitches on your needle?

Have you ever inadvertently increased the number of stitches on your needle? Beginners often make this mistake. One common error is knitting into both legs of the stitch below the first stitch on the needle after the first knit row. Another error is performing an unwanted yarn-over when moving the yarn from front to back.

Pick Up a Dropped Edge Stitch Several Rows Below

An edge stitch that has been dropped and allowed to run for several rows has a different appearance from a run down the interior of a piece of knitting. Instead of seeing a row of horizontal ladders, you see 2 loops at the edge: The dropped stitch and a large loop of yarn. For this repair, use a crochet hook in the appropriate size for your yarn.

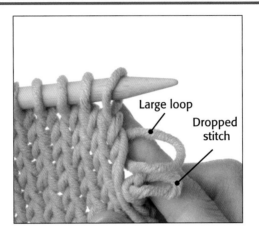

Large loop

Dropped stitch

1 Insert the crochet hook from front to back through the dropped stitch. Pull the big loop through the hook to the front.

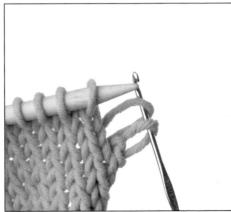

2 Repeat step 1 until you get to the top.

3 Use the hook to pull the working yarn through the last stitch that you created.

4 Use the hook to place the repaired stitch back onto the left needle.

The repaired stitch is ready to be worked as usual.

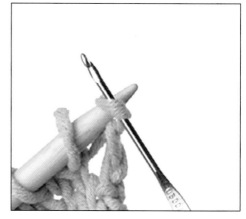

Unravel Stitch by Stitch

If you make an error that can't be fixed by using any of the previous methods, then you probably need to unravel some of your work. If it's on the same row that you're working on, you can unravel stitch by stitch. Once you become good at unraveling stitch by stitch, it will feel like you're knitting backward, or *unknitting*.

① On the knit side, hold the working yarn in back, and insert the left needle from front to back into the stitch in the row below the next stitch on the right needle.

② Drop the stitch above off the right needle and pull the working yarn to unknit it.

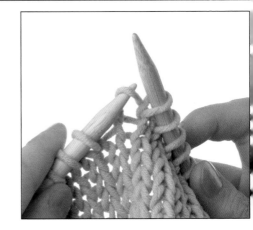

③ On the purl side, hold the working yarn in front and insert the left needle from front to back into the stitch in the row below the next stitch on the right needle.

④ Drop the stitch above off the right needle and pull the working yarn to unpurl it.

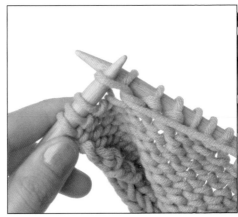

If you make an error that is more than 1 row down from where you are in your knitting, you need to unravel row by row.

1 Slide the stitches off the needle and pull the working yarn until you have unraveled the desired number of rows.

2 Using a needle that is smaller in diameter than the working needle, carefully slide the stitches back onto that needle. Take care not to twist the stitches when you put them back onto the needle.

You can now resume knitting with the working needles.

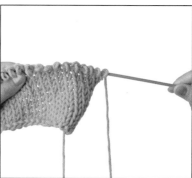

TIP

A Safer Way to Unravel

To avoid dropping stitches as you unravel, you can weave a needle that is smaller in diameter than the working needles in and out of the stitches in the row, below the point to which you would like to unravel. Be sure that the needle goes under the right side of each stitch and over the left side of each stitch. When the entire row is on the needle, pull the working yarn to unravel the rows above the needle. You can then resume knitting with the working needles.

chapter 6

Reading Written Instructions

You have probably looked into knitting books and thought, "Is this English?" Knitting instructions contain a lot of information in terms and formats that are unfamiliar and intimidating at first. This chapter will enable you to understand what you are reading the next time you look at a knitting pattern.

A knitting pattern contains all of the information you need to make the item: the sizes for dimensions to which the project can be knit, the materials and tools you need to make the project, special techniques used in the design, and the step-by-step instructions. The following should help you find your way through your next knitting pattern.

SKILL LEVEL

Some patterns list the skill level required for the project.

Beginner: Good for first-time knitters. Includes little shaping, and uses basic knit and purl stitches.

Easy: Still uses basic stitches or easy stitch pattern repeats, easy color work (like stripes), and easy shaping and finishing.

Intermediate: May include a few different stitch patterns, or simple lace, cables, or intarsia. Might involve using double-pointed needles or circular knitting. More advanced shaping and finishing than the previous level.

Experienced: Includes more complicated stitch patterns, sophisticated techniques, intricate color work (like fair isle), complex cables, lace, or intarsia, complicated or short row shaping.

SIZE

The size or sizes that a pattern can be knit for are represented by measurements: chest circumference for sweaters; height x width for scarves, blankets, bags, and shawls; or circumference for hats and skirts. Sometimes baby and kids' patterns will list the age range for the sizes, along with the measurements.

Many knitting patterns are written for more than one size, with the smallest size listed first, and the remaining sizes listed in parentheses—for example, S (M, L). Throughout the pattern, the instructions contain information pertaining to the various sizes, such as stitch counts and numbers of decreases or increases, using the same format. For example, a pattern written for S (M, L) could instruct you to cast on 40 (50, 60) stitches. That means if you're knitting the medium size, you cast on 50 stitches.

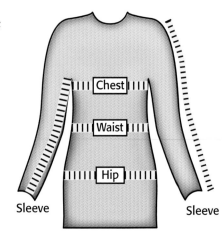

Chest

Waist

Hip

Sleeve

Sleeve

Some patterns also include *schematics*, or diagrams of the finished knit pieces, showing the measurements for each piece before finishing. Schematics are a helpful guide when you're knitting your pieces: You can measure your knitting as you go along, and compare it to the schematic to be sure you're on track.

MATERIALS

A list of materials usually follows the sizing information. This section includes everything you need to make the project: yarn type and amounts, all of the needles, tools, buttons, and any other items required.

GAUGE

Gauge, the number of stitches and rows per inch that you achieve with the yarn specified on the needle size indicated in the pattern, is given after the list of materials. Too much emphasis cannot be placed on the importance of achieving the correct gauge before beginning a new project. See the following page to learn about measuring gauge.

STITCH PATTERNS AND SPECIAL INSTRUCTIONS

The stitch patterns you use to make the project often appear just before the instructions. For example, if the project is worked in seed stitch, row-by-row instructions for how to work seed stitch would be under this heading. Any special instructions or notes, like, "this sweater is worked in the round up to the armholes and then worked back and forth after that" would appear here, too.

When you knit something where size and fit are crucial, you need to understand gauge. *Gauge* (referred to as *tension* in the UK) is the number of stitches and rows per inch that you get with a given yarn on a given size needle. Different yarns knit to different gauges, the same yarn knits to a different gauge on different sizes of needles, and different knitters knit the same yarn on the same needles at different gauges.

UNDERSTANDING GAUGE

A good knitting pattern specifies the gauge that is required to attain the desired size or fit of the garment. For example, it may read something like, "Gauge: 20 stitches and 30 rows to 4 inches over stockinette stitch on size 7 (4.5mm) needles." In order for you to create the sweater or hat so that it comes out in the same measurements that the pattern specifies and so that it fits properly, you must be sure that you are knitting to that same gauge. Although your yarn label should indicate what size needle to use with the yarn and what the desired gauge is, you should use that recommendation only as a guide, as tension varies from knitter to knitter.

These three swatches were all made using 20 stitches and 30 rows, but with different yarns and different needle sizes. You can see how varied the sizes of the final results are. That is why it is so important to use the same gauge that the pattern calls for—with the yarn that you have chosen for the project. Even a slight discrepancy can have a tremendous effect. A 1-stitch-per-inch difference in gauge, over a large number of stitches, can result in a final size that is several inches smaller or larger than desired.

Sometimes a knitting pattern will cite the gauge for a particular stitch pattern, if that is what is primarily used for that garment. Stitch pattern, like needle size and yarn type, can affect gauge. For example, the same yarn, worked in stockinette stitch on size 7 needles, knits to a different gauge in a ribbed pattern on the same needles.

UNDERSTANDING HOW GAUGE CAN DIFFER AMONG STITCH PATTERNS

These three swatches were all made from the same yarn and using the same needles, over 20 stitches and 30 rows, but with different stitch patterns. You can see how varied the sizes of the final results are. That is why it is important to knit up a gauge swatch in the stitch pattern that you're going to use for your garment.

Substituting a Stitch Pattern

If you want to substitute a stitch pattern for the one that is specified in a written pattern, it's easy to switch to one that knits to the same gauge. If that is not the case—and you're willing to rewrite the instructions yourself—then you will need to cast on fewer or more stitches, depending on how off-gauge you are. For example, if you're working from a hat pattern where the finished circumference is 20 inches and the gauge is 5 stitches per inch, then the pattern should indicate casting on 100 stitches. If your chosen stitch pattern gauge is 6 stitches per inch, then you'll have to cast on 120 stitches to make the same size hat. You'll also have to rewrite the shaping instructions to suit the new stitch count. That is why it is easier to substitute a stitch pattern that knits to the same gauge.

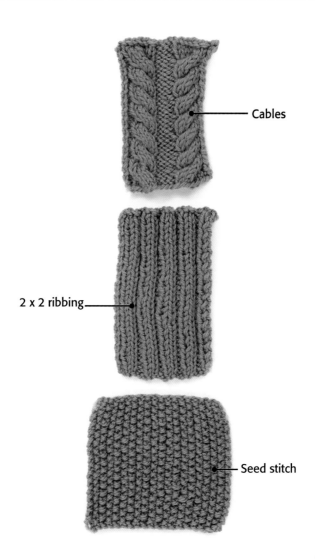

Cables

2 x 2 ribbing

Seed stitch

Make and Measure a Gauge Swatch

Before starting a project, *always* make a gauge swatch to ensure that you are knitting to the same gauge as the pattern. A gauge swatch is a small square of knitting that is used to measure how many stitches and rows per inch you are getting with a particular yarn on a certain size needle. It takes only a few minutes to make, and you will definitely not regret it. Many new knitters skip this step and spend hours on a sweater that ends up too big or too small.

To make a gauge swatch, you need to use the yarn and needle size that is specified in your pattern, and a stitch-and-needle gauge or tape measure. It is not a bad idea to have three pairs of needles handy: the size called for, the next size smaller, and the next size larger.

1. Cast on the same number of stitches that the pattern says is equal to 4 inches.

2. Work in stockinette stitch (Knit on the right side, purl on the wrong side) until the swatch is 4 inches long (measuring from the cast-on edge to the needle).

3. Bind off your stitches somewhat loosely, cut the working yarn (leaving about a 6-inch tail), and pull the tail through the last stitch.

4. Lay your swatch on a flat surface. Place your stitch and needle gauge (or other measuring device) so that the opening is centered both horizontally and vertically on the swatch.

5. Count how many stitches there are in the horizontal 2-inch space, and how many rows there are in the vertical 2-inch space.

6. Divide these numbers by 2. That is the number of stitches and rows that you are getting per inch.

   If your pattern lists gauge as a certain number of stitches and rows over 4 inches, then multiply your stitch and row counts for 2 inches by 2.

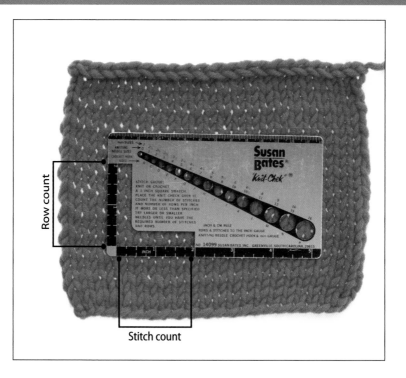

Row count

Stitch count

TIP

Not Getting the Right Gauge?

If you are getting more stitches per 4 inches than the pattern calls for, try switching to a needle that is one size larger. If you are getting fewer stitches per 4 inches than the pattern calls for, try switching to a needle that is one size smaller. Make a new gauge swatch and measure again. If necessary, go up or down another needle size, create a new swatch, and re-measure.

It is difficult to match both stitch and row gauge, but it is crucial to match the stitch gauge accurately. If the row gauge is slightly off, you can work in terms of the pattern's vertical measurements rather than its row counts.

Most knitting patterns are written for multiple sizes. Although sizes are often expressed in the general terms small, medium, and large, it is more important to look at the measurements given for each size, which usually represent the finished size of the garment. After you find that information, the best way to determine what size to knit is to take body measurements, if possible.

READING INSTRUCTIONS FOR SIZE

Patterns written for multiple sizes usually list the smallest size first, with the remaining sizes listed in parentheses—for example, S (M, L). Throughout the pattern, the instructions contain information pertaining to the various sizes, such as stitch counts and numbers of decreases or increases, using a parallel format. For example, a pattern written for S (M, L) may instruct you to cast on 50 (60, 70) stitches. That means that if you're knitting the medium size, you need to cast on 60 stitches. Some knitters avoid confusion by highlighting or underlining the part of the instructions that pertain to the size they are knitting.

CHOOSING A SIZE

Knitting patterns list the measurements relating to the sizes included in the instructions. These measurements usually indicate the finished sizes of the knitted garment. Different designers use unique templates based on their idea of what fits a certain age or size range; also, older books may have a completely different mode of sizing. As a result, the best way to figure out what size to knit for yourself or for someone else is to take body measurements, if possible. Then you can decide whether you want the garment to have a loose, comfortable fit, or a snug, tailored fit. You then check your measurements against the pattern's finished measurements and make your choice.

| Actual Body Measurement | Finished Measurements | | | | |
Chest	Tight Fit	Tailored Fit	Normal Fit	Loose Fit	Oversized Fit
31–32 in.	30 in.	32 in.	34 in.	36 in.	37–38 in.
33–34 in.	32 in.	34 in.	36 in.	38 in.	39–40 in.
35–36 in.	34 in.	36 in.	38 in.	40 in.	41–42 in.
37–38 in.	36 in.	38 in.	40 in.	42 in.	43–44 in.
39–40 in.	38 in.	40 in.	42 in.	44 in.	45–46 in.

READING SCHEMATICS

Schematics are diagrams of the finished knit pieces for a project. They indicate the measurements for each piece before everything has been sewn together. Schematics are a very handy reference. You can measure as you knit by comparing it to the schematics, making sure that you're coming up with the same thing. If your row gauge is slightly off, you can follow the schematic instead of the instructions' row counts to ensure that your pieces will be the correct length. The measurements listed on schematics do not include embellishments such as collars, button bands, or decorative edgings that are added later.

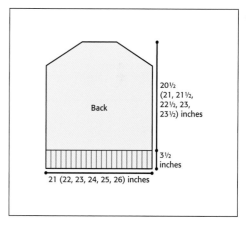

Back

20½ (21, 21½, 22½, 23, 23½) inches

3½ inches

21 (22, 23, 24, 25, 26) inches

CONTINUED ON NEXT PAGE

MEASURING YOUR KNITTING

You should measure your knitting frequently to ensure that your gauge is correct. To measure, lay your knitted piece out on a flat, smooth surface; do not stretch, distort, or scrunch it up. Measure width at the widest point, as the area near the ribbing or the needle will not give the most accurate reading. Measure length at the center from the lower edge to just under the knitting needle.

For shaped areas, like sleeves and armholes, measure between the dotted lines indicated on the diagrams below.

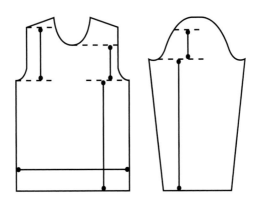

If what you are knitting includes color work, textured stitches, or cables, chances are that your pattern includes a knitting chart. Don't be put off by all of the symbols and hieroglyphics that you see there; most patterns provide a key to all of the symbols used in each chart.

READING A CHART IN THE RIGHT DIRECTION

A square in a knitting chart represents a stitch; a horizontal row of squares represents a row. You read a chart as you work the knitting: from bottom to top and starting at the lower-right corner. The first horizontal row of squares represents a right-side row (unless otherwise specified) and is read from right to left. The second horizontal row, a wrong-side row, is read from left to right. (For circular knitting, all chart rows are read from right to left.) Most charts represent only a partial section of the knitting that is repeated to create the overall pattern. As a result, after you work the last stitch in a chart row, you return to the beginning of the same chart row and repeat. Working row-wise is the same: After you work the last row of the chart, you repeat the chart from the bottom.

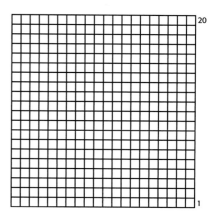

CONTINUED ON NEXT PAGE

READING A COLOR CHART

When a chart is used to represent a color pattern, each square is filled with a particular color or a symbol that corresponds with the color of yarn in which that stitch and/or row should be worked. You read this type of chart as described on the previous page: from bottom to top and back and forth, starting with the lower-right corner.

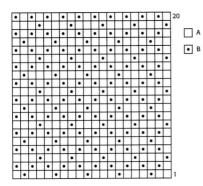

☐ A

⊡ B

TIP

Keeping Track of Where You Left Off

It's easy to forget where you left off when you set your knitting aside. Using a row counter is a good way to easily keep track of where you are in your stitch pattern or shaping. If you don't have one handy, you can use sticky notes to keep a record. Just adhere the note to your knitting instructions, and throw it away when it's no longer relevant.

READING A STITCH PATTERN CHART

When a chart is used to represent a textured stitch pattern, each square is either empty or contains a symbol. Symbols vary from pattern to pattern. For simple knit-and-purl patterns, an empty square means, "knit on the right-side rows and purl on the wrong-side rows." A square that contains a dot means, "purl on the right-side rows and knit on the wrong-side rows." More complex stitch patterns, such as cable patterns, contain many symbols representing different techniques.

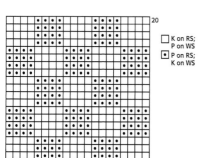

□ K on RS;
P on WS
⊡ P on RS;
K on WS

TIP

Turn It Upside-Down for Socks and Top-Down Items

Socks, mittens, gloves, and some hats and sweaters are worked from the top down. If you work color patterns directly from a stitch pattern chart that is meant for an item that is knit from the bottom up, the pattern or motif will be upside-down. To work one of these motifs or patterns properly, turn the chart upside-down.

chapter 7

Stitch Patterns and Maneuvers

You can mix knit and purl stitches to create eye-catching patterns and three-dimensional textures. You form some pattern stitches simply by knitting a certain number of stitches and purling a certain number of stitches for a certain number of rows. Other patterns, like highly textured fabrics or cables, call for stitch maneuvers: twisting stitches, and moving stitches sideways, up, or down.

Simple Stitch Patterns

Here are a few of the simplest and most common stitch patterns.

GARTER STITCH

Garter stitch is the easiest stitch pattern, and it always lies flat. It looks exactly the same on the front and the back.

① Row 1: Knit.

② Repeat row 1. After you knit several rows, you see horizontal ridges appear. Two knit rows form one ridge.

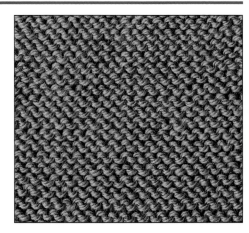

STOCKINETTE STITCH AND REVERSE STOCKINETTE STITCH

Stockinette stitch is the pattern that is most often used for sweaters. It looks like rows of flat V's on the front (the right side), and rows of bumps on the back (the wrong side). Reverse stockinette stitch is the same as regular stockinette, only the bumpy side is considered the right side.

① Row 1 (right side): Knit.

② Row 2 (wrong side): Purl.

③ Repeat rows 1–2.

Note: Work the same for reverse stockinette stitch, only label row 1 as the wrong side, and row 2 as the right side.

1 X 1 RIB

For 1 x 1 rib, cast on an odd number of stitches. To keep the pattern correct, be sure to knit the stitches that look like V's and purl the stitches that look like bumps. This rib is commonly used on jacket cuffs, and it also works well for scarves.

1. Row 1 (right side): Knit 1, *purl 1, knit 1; repeat from * to the end of the row.

2. Row 2 (wrong side): Purl 1, *knit 1, purl 1; repeat from * to the end of the row.

3. Repeat rows 1-2.

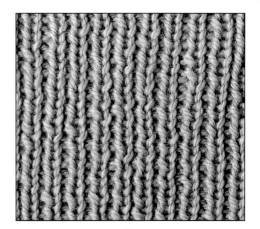

SEED STITCH

Seed stitch creates a nice bumpy-textured fabric that lies flat and looks the same on both sides. You knit the purl stitches and purl the knit stitches. When using seed stitch, you need to cast on an even number of stitches.

1. Row 1 (right side): *Knit 1, purl 1; repeat from * to the end of the row.

2. Row 2 (wrong side): *Purl 1, knit 1; repeat from * to the end of the row.

3. Repeat rows 1-2.

TIP

Counting Rows in a Stitch Pattern?

It's pretty easy to count rows in stockinette stitch, because you can just point the tip of your needle into the center of each V on the front and count upward. When stitches are difficult to count, the best solution is to slip a row counter onto your needle and diligently keep track that way. Doing so can save you a lot of time because you do not have to keep counting over and over again.

Selvages are edge stitches that are worked differently from the body of a piece of knitting. They create a stable, even edge that makes seaming easier, or that forms a firm, attractive finished border. Selvages also help when you don't want part of your stitch pattern to disappear into the seam.

GARTER STITCH SELVAGE

Knitting the first and last stitch of every row, and working the pattern stitch—in this case, stockinette stitch—in between forms a garter stitch selvage. It looks slightly different on the right side versus the left side. You use this selvage technique on the edges of a sweater back or pullover front to make seaming easy; you can also use it to add a tidy edge on a scarf or blanket.

1. Row 1: Knit 1 (this is a selvage stitch), work across the row to the last stitch, knit 1 (this is also a selvage stitch).

2. Row 2: Repeat row 1.

3. Repeat rows 1–2 to work selvages on each edge.

SLIP-STITCH SELVAGE

This selvage forms a neat and attractive chain along the side. You can use it decoratively, but it also works well for seaming or as a pick-up row for other edgings.

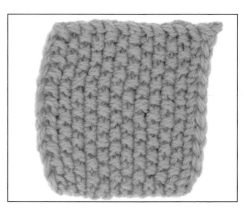

1. Row 1 (right side): Slip 1 knitwise (this is a selvage stitch), work across the row to the last stitch, slip 1 knitwise (this is also a selvage stitch).

2. Row 2 (wrong side): Purl 1 (selvage), work across the row to the last stitch, purl 1.

3. Repeat rows 1–2 to work selvages on each edge.

Bobbles

Bobbles add a playful three-dimensional accent to your knitting. You can use bobbles for effect in many ways: as a single row along a border, repeated in an allover pattern, or placed inside cables.

Many bobble-making methods involve knitting several times into one stitch, turning the work and working the new stitches, and then turning it back again. The method shown here is easy and doesn't require turning. The abbreviation for make a bobble is mb.

① Work to the point where you want the bobble. Knit into the front, back, front, back, and front (that's five times) of the next stitch.

② Without turning the work, use the left needle to pick up the fourth stitch and pass it over the fifth and off the needle; pass the third stitch over the fifth and off the needle; pass the second stitch over the fifth and off the needle; and finally, pass the first stitch over the fifth and off the needle.

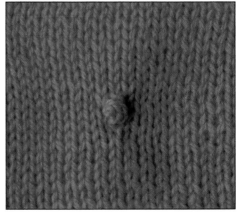

Knit One in the Row Below

You have probably come across the direction, "knit 1 stitch in the row below" before; it is often used in textured stitch patterns, because it causes the fabric to pucker slightly.

① Holding the working yarn at the back, insert the right needle from front to back into the stitch, directly below the next stitch on the left needle.

Note: Be sure to insert the needle all the way through to the back before knitting, so that the stitch above becomes caught up by the new stitch.

② Wrap the working yarn around the tip of the right needle and knit as usual, sliding the stitch above off the left needle at the same time.

Knit or Purl Through Back of Loop

A common direction in knitting patterns is "k1 tbl" or "knit 1 through back of loop." Likewise, you often see "p1 tbl" or "purl 1 through back of loop." Knitting or purling through the back loop twists the stitch, and so it is a frequently used maneuver in textured, twist-stitch patterns. It is also used in the bar increase, where you knit into the front and back of the same stitch. You also find "tbl" in the decreases k2tog tbl and p2tog tbl.

KNIT THROUGH BACK OF LOOP

1 Holding the working yarn at the back, insert the right needle knitwise, from front to back, into the back loop of the next knit stitch on the left needle.

2 Wrap the working yarn around the tip of the right needle and knit as usual.

PURL THROUGH BACK OF LOOP

1 Holding the working yarn at the front, insert the right needle purlwise, from back to front, into the back loop of the next purl stitch on the left needle.

2 Wrap the working yarn around the tip of the right needle and purl as usual.

Simple Cables

Cables look more complicated than they actually are. You make basic cables by holding one or more stitches on a cable needle to the front or the back of your work, knitting the next one or more stitches from the left needle, and then knitting the stitches from the cable needle. Whether you hold the stitches to the back or front determines which direction the cable crosses.

To practice the following cables, cast 16 stitches of smooth yarn onto your knitting needles, and have a cable needle ready.

SIMPLE BACK CROSS CABLE

1. Row 1 (right side): Purl 5, knit 6, purl 5.

2. Rows 2 and 4 (wrong side): Knit 5, purl 6, knit 5.

3. Row 3 (cable row): Purl 5, slip the next 3 stitches to a cable needle as if to purl, and hold at the back of the work (a).

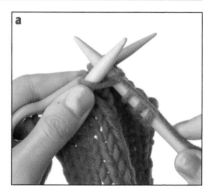

4. Knit the next 3 stitches from the left needle. Now use the right needle to knit the 3 stitches from the cable needle, starting with the first stitch that was slipped onto the needle (b), purl 5.

5. Row 4: Repeat row 2.

6. Repeat rows 1–4.

TIP

Quick Cable Knitting Tip

If knitting directly from the cable needle feels awkward, try slipping the held stitches back to the left needle, without twisting, before knitting them.

SIMPLE FRONT CROSS CABLE

1. Row 1 (right side): Purl 5, knit 6, purl 5.

2. Row 2 (wrong side): Knit 5, purl 6, knit 5.

3. Row 3 (cable row): Purl 5, slip the next 3 stitches to a cable needle as if to purl, and hold at the front of the work (a).

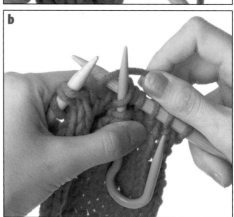

4. Knit the next 3 stitches from the left needle. Now use the right needle to knit the 3 stitches from the cable needle, starting with the first stitch that was slipped onto the needle (b), purl 5.

5. Row 4: Repeat row 2.

6. Repeat rows 1–4.

TIP

Which Cable Needle Is Best?

There are several types of cable needles. Some look like small double-pointed needles, while others look like hooks. The tiny double-pointed type is easy to knit from directly. The hook style holds the stitches without slipping out, and stays out of your way. Experiment with all kinds of cable needles to find your match. As to size, use a cable needle that is slightly smaller in diameter than your working knitting needle. A cable needle that is too thick will stretch out your stitches.

chapter 8

Knitting in the Round

Knitting in the round, or circular knitting, is what you do when you want to knit a tube. Hats, socks, mittens, gloves, and skirts are frequently knit in the round. When you knit in the round, you knit around and around on the right side only. Therefore, if you're working in stockinette stitch, knitting in the round eliminates the need to purl. It also reduces the necessity of sewing seams, so that finishing is quicker and easier.

Circular Knitting Basics

Circular knitting intimidates some knitters because the needles look unfamiliar. However, knitting in the round is in many ways simpler than flat knitting, and it requires less finishing skill. If you haven't already, you should give circular knitting a try.

USES FOR, AND ADVANTAGES OF, CIRCULAR KNITTING

Circular knitting is great for making hats, mittens, socks, gloves, and a lot of other things. You can also knit certain sweaters in the round. Because most items that are knit in the round are worked in one piece, the need for extensive finishing, seaming, and weaving-in of ends is diminished. Another benefit is that you're always working from the right side: As a result, stranded color knitting and elaborate stitch patterns are easier to follow continuously.

NEEDLE TYPES AND LENGTHS FOR CIRCULAR KNITTING

You can knit in the round on circular needles or on sets of double-pointed needles. Circular needles, which come in a variety of materials and lengths, are basically needle tips connected by a plastic or nylon cord. Whether you use wood, metal, or plastic is up to you. The circumference of what you are going to knit determines what length of needle you can use; your pattern should specify that length. Before circular needles were invented, people knit in the round on double-pointed needles. Today, double-pointed needles are used mainly for smaller items, like hats and socks. They are sold in sets of four or five. If you're knitting an item that starts out with a circumference wide enough for a circular needle, but decreases to a circumference too short for a circular needle, then you can change from the circular needle to double-pointed needles at that point in the project.

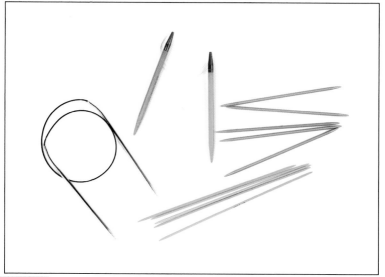

TIP

Double-Pointed Needles Too Slippery?
Slippery metal double-pointed needles can produce a lot of dropped stitches. Try using bamboo or wood double-pointed needles when knitting socks, mittens, and gloves. These needles won't slip out of your stitches as readily, and you'll have more control.

CONTINUED ON NEXT PAGE

MARKING AND KEEPING TRACK OF ROUNDS AND PATTERN REPEATS

Some knitters struggle to keep track of where they are in a *pattern repeat*, or how many rounds have been worked with circular knitting. There are many useful tools to assist you, as well as indicators in the actual knitting. To keep track of the beginning and end of the round, use a split ring marker or knotted loop of scrap yarn to indicate the first stitch of the round. If you lose the marker, the location of the tail that is left over from casting on is also a good indicator of the join. Row counters are helpful in recording the number of rounds that are knit. If your project involves stitch patterns and cable panels, you can mark the beginning and end of repeats with split ring markers. Attach them to the first and last stitch of the repeat.

GAUGE IN CIRCULAR KNITTING

If the fit is crucial, then you should make a swatch that reflects your in-the-round gauge. Some knitters, particularly Continental-method knitters, achieve a tighter gauge in circular knitting than they do in flat knitting, due to purl stitches in flat knitting coming out looser than knit stitches. To make a swatch that reflects your circular knitting gauge, use two double-pointed needles the same size that you are going to use for the body of your project. Cast onto one double-pointed needle the equivalent of 4 or 5 inches worth of stitches, and then knit 1 row with the second double-pointed needle. Instead of turning the work and purling the next row, bring the working yarn very loosely from the end of the row back to the beginning of the row, still with the right side facing. Knit another row. Continue working in this manner, knitting each row beginning at the same end, and draping the working yarn across the back between rows until your swatch is approximately square. Measure your gauge as usual.

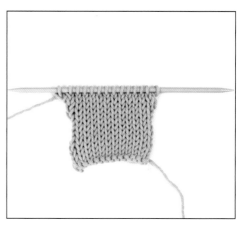

TIP

Closing the Gap

Many knitters complain of a ladder of loose stitches along the vertical line where the two needles come together in circular knitting. With circular needles, this occurs only along the join of the round, but on double-pointed needles, it can appear between each needle. To improve the appearance of the stitches that lie at the beginning and end of the needles, be sure to tug firmly on the working yarn when knitting the first 2 stitches on a new needle, and hold the right needle securely up against the left needle when knitting these 2 stitches.

Cast On with Circular Needles

Choose a circular needle that is the appropriate diameter for your yarn, and that is at least 2 or 3 inches shorter than the circumference of the item that you're going to knit. If the needle is too long, you won't be able to join the round. You can use a circular needle that is much shorter than—even half—the circumference of your knitting. However, a needle that is too short will make it difficult to see your knitting, because it will be so gathered.

1 Cast on stitches in the same manner that you would with straight needles, using the method of your choice.

Note: *If the cast-on stitches do not spread easily around the entire needle and cannot be joined into a round, try a shorter needle.*

2 When you have cast on the correct number of stitches, make sure that your stitches are not twisted.

Note: *To avoid twisted stitches, make sure that the cast-on edge is going around the inside of the needle.*

TIP

The Best Cast-On Methods for Circular Knitting

You can use your preferred cast-on method for circular knitting. However, some cast-ons are better than others. For example, the simple cast-on is thin and tends to spiral around the needle easily, which could lead to creating an unwanted twist in your knit tube. The most reliable cast-ons for circular knitting are the long-tail method, or the knit cast-on.

Knit Using Circular Needles

When you knit on circular needles, you knit in rounds, not rows. Every round is a right side row, so if you're working in stockinette stitch, you do not have to purl.

Take care not to let the stitches get twisted before joining your round. If they are twisted and you knit a few rounds, the entire piece of knitting will be twisted. The only way to correct this is to unravel all the way back to the cast-on row.

① In your right hand, hold the end of the needle to which working yarn is attached. Place a marker after the last stitch that was cast on to mark the end of the round.

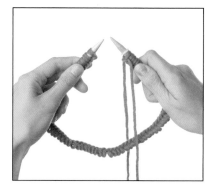

② Use the needle in your right hand to knit the first cast-on stitch from the needle in your left hand, giving the yarn a firm tug (on this first stitch only) so that the join is snug.

Knitting the first stitch joins the round.

③ Knit until you reach the marker. To begin the second round, slip the marker from the left needle to the right needle, and knit the first stitch as in step 2.

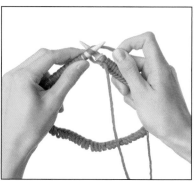

TIP

Fixing a Stiff Circular Needle Cord

If the cord on your circular needle is curly and hard to manage, try immersing it in hot water for a minute or two, and then straighten it. Heating it—not melting it—for 15–20 seconds with a blow dryer also works.

Just like casting on with circular needles, you must avoid twisting the stitches when casting on to double-pointed needles. The difference is that you divide the cast-on stitches over three needles.

1 With four double-pointed needles, cast on all of the stitches that are called for onto one double-pointed needle. Then slip one-third of the stitches onto a second needle, and one-third onto a third needle.

Note: If the stitches cannot be divided equally in thirds, you can approximate the amount.

2 Arrange the three needles so that they form a triangle: The needle with the working yarn attached should be the right side of the tri-angle (a), the center needle should be the base of the triangle (b), and the needle with the first cast-on stitch should be the left side of the triangle (c).

Note: Make sure that the cast-on edge is running around the center of the triangle, untwisted.

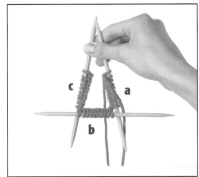

TIP

What if all of the stitches won't fit on one double-pointed needle when casting on?

If you are casting on too many stitches to fit on one double-pointed needle in step 1, use a long single-pointed needle to cast on all of the stitches. Then slip them on to the double-pointed needles, dividing them as evenly as possible.

Knit Using Double-Pointed Needles

Knitting on double-pointed needles can feel awkward at first, but once you work a few rounds, it will all come together. It is really the best way to knit mittens and gloves, and so it's worth giving this type of knitting a try.

1. Make sure that the needles are facing you, with the needle with the working yarn attached to it on the right. Place a marker after the last stitch that was cast on to mark the end of the round. In your left hand, hold the needle with the first cast-on stitch on it.

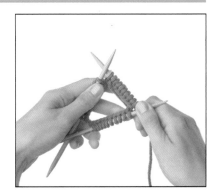

2. Using your empty fourth needle, join the round by knitting the first cast-on stitch from the left needle; give the yarn a firm tug (on this first stitch only) so that the join is snug.

   Knitting the first stitch joins the round.

3. Knit until you reach the marker. To begin the second round, slip the marker from the left needle to the right needle, and knit the first stitch as in step 2.

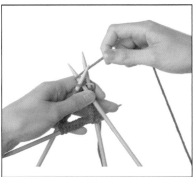

If you don't like knitting on double-pointed needles, you can knit small-circumference items like socks, legwarmers, mittens, and hats on two circular needles. To practice this method, you'll need a ball of yarn and two circular needles in the diameter recommended for your yarn. The needles don't have to be the same length.

① Cast on at least 30 stitches on one of the circular needles.

② Slip half of the stitches onto the second circular needle.

③ Slide each set of stitches to the other end of its circular needle, as shown. Arrange the needles so that the working yarn is coming from the needle in your right hand.

Note: *Take care not to twist the point where the cast-on stitches split onto the two needles.*

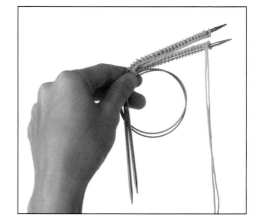

④ Slide the stitches on the needle with the working yarn attached so that they are positioned on the flexible cable section of the needle. Drop that needle and hold the empty end of the needle holding the first half of the stitches in your right hand, ready to knit.

⑤ Use the needle end in your right hand to knit the first stitch on the left needle, giving the working yarn a firm tug to close the round.

Knitting this first stitch joins the round.

⑥ Knit the rest of the first half of the stitches from the left needle, and slide these worked stitches to the flexible cable section of the needle. Drop that needle.

⑦ Slide the unworked stitches to the tip of their needle so that the cast-on tail is at the bottom and the next stitch of the round is ready to be worked.

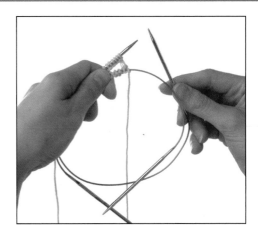

⑧ Use the empty end of the needle holding the unworked stitches to knit the rest of the stitches to complete the round.

⑨ Repeat steps 4–8.

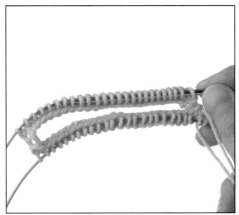

You can translate knitting instructions that are written for flat knitting so that they work for circular knitting. Just remember to work your circular gauge swatch as described on p. 87.

Certain patterns, like those involving intarsia, can't be easily converted to circular knitting. Take some time to experiment before jumping into a big project. Refer to the Appendix for the knitting abbreviations used in this section.

RIGHT SIDE VERSUS WRONG SIDE

Before

Rows 1 and 3 (RS): P2, *k3, p2; rep from * to end.

Rows 2, 4 and 6 (WS): K2, *p3, k2; rep from * to end.

Row 5: P2, yo, sl 1, k2tog, psso, yo, p2; rep from * to end.

Rep rows 1–6 for bell rib.

After

Rnds 1–4: *K3, p2; rep from * to end.

Rnd 5: *Yo, sl1, k2tog, psso, yo, p2; rep from * to end.

Rnd 6: *K3, p2; rep from * to end.

Rep rounds 1–6 for bell rib.

Note: *The 2 extra stitches for centering the pattern when working flat are eliminated when working in the round.*

Remember that when you are working in the round, all rows—rounds, actually—are right-side, or RS, rows. As a result, when you rewrite your pattern, all right-side rows can be worked in the round as they are written, as long as you eliminate any stitches that may have been added outside the pattern repeat as selvages. For a wrong-side, or WS, row, keep in mind the following:

- Purl stitches on the WS are knit stitches on the RS.
- Read written instructions backward—from the end of the WS row to the beginning of the WS row—and write them out so that you do not become confused. For example, if the WS row reads, "Knit 1, purl 4," rewrite it as "Knit 4, purl 1."
- Read all rows of charted patterns from right to left.
- For WS instructions that say "with yarn in back," or wyib, substitute "with yarn in front," or wyif, and vice versa.

REWRITING FLAT INSTRUCTIONS TO CIRCULAR

Before beginning, you should convert your flat instructions into circular instructions in writing, because it's easy to lose track of where you are. See the sample conversion below for help.

Before	Row 1 (RS): *K1, p3: rep from * to end of row. Row 2 (WS): *K1, sl 1 wyib, k1, p1; rep from * to end of row.
After	Rnd 1: *K1, p3; rep from * to end of rnd. Rnd 2: *K1, p1, sl 1 wyif, p1; rep from * to end of rnd.

TIP

Joining the Round Invisibly

Knitting in the round is really like knitting in a spiral. That's why you get that little stair step when you join the round. You can alleviate this problem somewhat. When casting on, cast on 1 extra stitch. When you join the first round, slip the last stitch that was cast on from the right needle to the left. Join the round using both the working yarn and the tail to knit the first 2 stitches on the left needle together (these are the extra stitch that you slipped from right to left, and what had been the first cast-on stitch). Drop the tail and knit the rest of the round as usual. To begin the second round, knit together that first double stitch made from the working yarn and the tail. You will now be back to the required number of stitches.

Work Seamless Stripes in the Round

Because circular knitting is actually knitting a spiral, lining up stripes at the beginning or end of each new round can be tricky. You end up with a little stair step where the old round ends and the new round begins.

Some knitters accept the stair step as a matter of course, which is fine. However, if you find this little imperfection undesirable, you can try the following to diminish the stair step.

1 After you finish the first color stripe, change to the new color at the beginning of the round and knit 1 round.

2 Before knitting the first stitch of the next round (the second round of the new color), lift the stitch below the first stitch (in the old color) and put it onto the left needle ahead of the first stitch of the next round.

3 Knit the 2 stitches together and complete the round as usual.

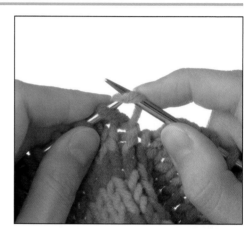

4 Repeat steps 1–3.

Simple Stitch Patterns in the Round

You work common stitch patterns like garter stitch and stockinette stitch differently in the round than you do flat, as discussed on p. 74–75. Here's a handy guide to working the most frequently used stitch patterns in the round.

GARTER STITCH (A)

1 Round 1: Knit.
2 Round 2: Purl.
3 Repeat rounds 1–2.

STOCKINETTE STITCH (B)

1 Round 1: Purl.
2 Repeat round 1.

Note: For stockinette stitch, knit every round.

1 X 1 RIB (C)

For 1 x 1 rib in the round, cast on an even number of stitches.

1 Round 1: *Knit 1, purl 1; repeat from * to the end of the round.
2 Repeat round 1.

SEED STITCH (D)

For seed stitch in the round, it's best to cast on an odd number of stitches.

1 Round 1: Knit 1, *purl 1, knit 1; repeat from * to the end of the round.
2 Round 2: Purl 1, *knit 1, purl 1; repeat from * to the end of the round.
3 Repeat rounds 1–2.

Shaping

Without shaping, all knitting would be just rectangles. There are countless shaping options and techniques that you can use. To make your knitting wider, you need to increase, or add, a stitch or stitches. To make your knitting narrower, you need to decrease, or subtract, a stitch or stitches. This chapter contains a wealth of useful shaping methods.

A bar increase creates a visible horizontal bar of yarn where the increase is made. Knit 1 or 2 stitches at the beginning of the row before making a bar increase.

1 Insert the right needle into the next stitch and knit it, but do not bring the old stitch up and off the left needle; then insert the right needle into the back of the same stitch, as shown, and knit it again.

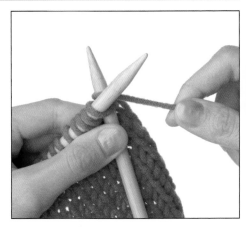

2 Bring the stitch that you knit into twice off the left needle.

You should now have 2 new stitches on the right needle: the one that you knit into the front of the stitch and the one that you knit into the back of it.

A yarn-over is an increase that is often used decoratively and for lacy patterns because it makes a hole. Here is how to perform a yarn-over increase on the knit side and on the purl side.

YARN-OVER WITH KNIT STITCH

① Bring the working yarn to the front of the needles, and lay it over the right needle from front to back.

② Knit the next stitch.

Laying the yarn over the right needle creates another stitch. On the next row, knit or purl it as usual.

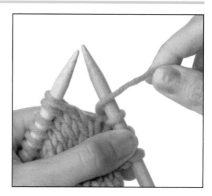

YARN-OVER WITH PURL STITCH

① Start with the working yarn at the front of the needles, wrap it over and under the right needle, and bring it back to the front.

② Purl the next stitch.

Laying the yarn over the right needle creates another stitch. On the next row, just knit it or purl it as usual.

TIP

Another Increase that Makes a Hole

The hole made with this increase is smaller than the yarn-over hole, and appears in the row below the row that you work it on. All you do is pick up the horizontal bar between the last stitch that you worked on the right needle and the next stitch to be worked on the left needle; you do this by inserting the left needle from front to back under the horizontal bar. Then knit into the front of this picked-up strand; you now see a little hole, and you have an extra stitch.

You can work yarn-overs into knit and purl stitches and at the beginnings of knit and purl rows. How you perform the yarn-over depends on what stitches come before and after it.

YARN-OVER BETWEEN A KNIT AND A PURL STITCH

1 After the knit stitch, bring the working yarn from the back to the front. Wrap it over and under the right needle and bring it back to the front.

2 Purl the next stitch.

YARN-OVER BETWEEN A PURL AND A KNIT STITCH

1 After the purl stitch, keep the working yarn at the front of the needles and lay it over the right needle from front to back.

2 Knit the next stitch.

MULTIPLE YARN-OVERS

1 After a knit or purl stitch, wrap yarn around the right needle as you would for 1 yarn-over.

2 Wrap the yarn around the right needle again.

You now have 2 yarn-overs on your right needle.

3 Repeat step 2 until you have the number of yarn-overs on your right needle that your pattern indicates.

AT THE BEGINNING OF A ROW

1 Keep the working yarn at the front of the needles. Insert the right needle knitwise into the first stitch of the new row on the left needle.

2 Lay the working yarn over the right needle from front to back.

Laying the working yarn over the right needle is the yarn-over.

3 Securing the yarn-over on the right needle with your thumb or forefinger, knit the next stitch.

Note: To perform a yarn-over at the beginning of a purl row, keep the working yarn at the back of the needles, and insert the right needle purlwise into the first stitch and purl it.

The make 1 increase is barely visible on the right side of your knitting. It involves lifting the horizontal strand between 2 stitches up onto the left needle and knitting it. You can make the increase slant to the right or to the left, depending on how you lift the horizontal strand.

RIGHT-SLANTING MAKE 1

① Before the next stitch, use the left needle to pick up the horizontal strand *from back to front* between the last stitch worked on the right needle and the next stitch to be worked on the left needle.

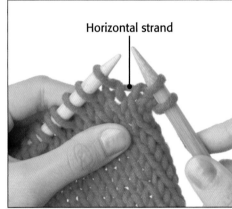

Horizontal strand

② Insert the right needle into the front of the strand and knit it.

Note: *The photo shows a right-slanting make 1 on the knit side. Working it on the purl side is technically the same: The horizontal strand is lifted onto the left needle from back to front and is purled in the front.*

LEFT-SLANTING MAKE 1

1 Before the next stitch, use the left needle to pick up the horizontal strand *from front to back* between the last stitch worked on the right needle and the next stitch to be worked on the left needle.

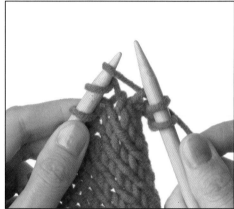

2 Insert the right needle into the back of the loop as shown, and knit it.

Note: *The photo shows a left-slanting make 1 on the knit side. Working it on the purl side is technically the same: The horizontal strand is lifted onto the left needle from front to back and is purled in the back of the loop.*

TIP

Positioning Increases Neatly

When instructions say, "Increase 1 stitch at the beginning of the row," you can do just that; however, it is neater to position increases (and decreases for that matter) 2 or 3 stitches in from the edges. For example, if your instructions say to increase 1 stitch at each end of a row, you can work the first 2 stitches, perform the increase, work until 2 stitches remain on the right needle, perform the increase, and work the last 2 stitches. Your edges will be tidy this way.

This useful increase is practically imperceptible. It's a good all-around increase that works well for shaping just about any knitted item. It can be worked on either the knit side or the purl side.

LIFTED INCREASE: KNIT SIDE

① Insert the right needle from front to back into the back loop of the stitch below the next stitch on the left needle (a), and knit it (b).

Note: In order to access the back of the stitch below the next stitch on the left needle, you need to rotate the left needle toward you so that the backs of the knit stitches are visible.

② Knit the next stitch.

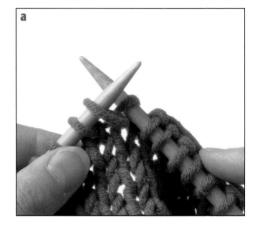

LIFTED INCREASE: PURL SIDE

1. Insert the right needle purlwise into the loop of the stitch below the next stitch on the left needle (a), and purl it (b).

2. Purl the next stitch.

Multiple Increases

Sometimes you need to increase more than one stitch at a time to achieve symmetrical shaping, or more pronounced shaping. Here are some double increase techniques, and some pointers on increasing many stitches at once.

DOUBLE BAR INCREASE

1. Working on the right side, knit across to the stitch *before* the center stitch of the row (known as the *axis stitch*) and then work a bar increase. (See p. 100.)

2. Work a second bar increase into the center stitch. Knit to the end of the row.

   Even though the second increase is worked on the axis stitch, the bar appears after it.

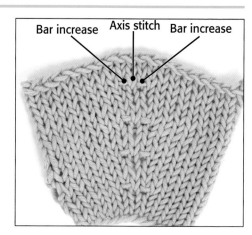

Bar increase   Axis stitch   Bar increase

DOUBLE MAKE 1 INCREASE

1. Working on the right side, knit across to the axis stitch. Perform a right-slanting make 1 increase, using the horizontal strand between the last stitch worked and the axis stitch.

2. Knit the axis stitch.

3. Perform a left-slanting make 1 increase (see p. 105 for instructions), using the horizontal strand between the axis stitch and the next stitch to be worked on the left needle. Knit to the end of the row.

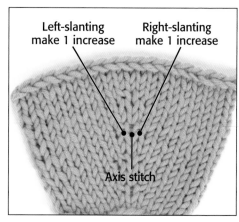

Left-slanting make 1 increase   Right-slanting make 1 increase

Axis stitch

DOUBLE YARN-OVER INCREASE

1. Knit across to the axis stitch and yarn over.
2. Knit the axis stitch.
3. Yarn over and knit to the end of the row.

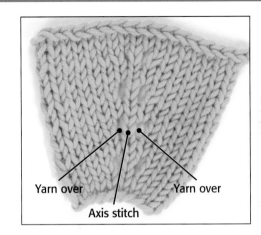

Yarn over

Yarn over

Axis stitch

INCREASING BY CASTING ON STITCHES

1. To cast on stitches at the beginning of a row, before working the row, use the simple cast-on method (see p. 17) and the working yarn to cast on the number of stitches required.
2. Knit the newly cast-on stitches as usual.

These are two of the most common decreases. The knit 2 together (k2tog) is performed with knit stitches, or in a stitch pattern where a knit stitch is required. The purl 2 together (p2tog) is performed with purl stitches, or in a stitch pattern where a purl stitch is required. Both decreases can be used at any point in a row of knitting or purling. This decrease, either knit or purled, slants somewhat to the right on the front side of your knitting.

KNIT 2 TOGETHER

1. Insert the right needle into the front of the next 2 stitches (as if to knit) on the left needle.
2. Wrap the yarn around the right needle and knit the 2 stitches as 1 stitch.

PURL 2 TOGETHER

1. Insert the right needle from back to front into the front of the next 2 stitches (as if to purl) on the left needle.
2. Wrap the yarn around the right needle and purl the 2 stitches as 1 stitch.

These two decreases are similar to the regular knit 2 together and purl 2 together decreases, only the 2 stitches are worked together through the backs of the loops instead of through the fronts. Both result in a left-slanting decrease on the front side of a piece of knitting. They are also referred to as k2tog tbl or p2tog tbl.

1 Insert the right needle from front to back into the back of the next 2 stitches on the left needle.

2 Knit the 2 stitches together as 1 stitch.

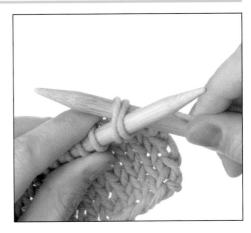

3 Insert the right needle from back to front into the back of the next 2 stitches on the left needle.

4 Purl the 2 stitches together as 1 stitch.

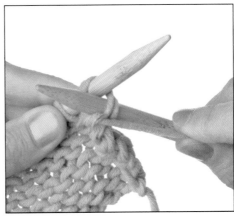

This decrease, abbreviated as ssk, is practically invisible. It is worked on the front side of a piece of knitting, and it slants to the left. If you want to shape your knitting on both sides symmetrically, you can begin the row with a slip, slip, knit and end the row with a knit 2 together. (See the tip on p. 105 about positioning increases and decreases neatly.)

1 Insert the right needle from front to back into the front (knitwise) of the next stitch on the left needle, and slip it onto the right needle.

2 Repeat step 1.

You have now slipped 2 stitches knitwise from the left needle to the right needle.

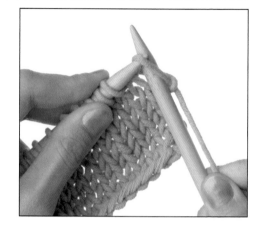

3 Insert the left needle from left to right into the fronts of both slipped stitches, and knit them as 1 stitch.

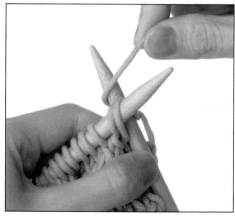

This decrease, which is also worked on the front side of a piece of knitting, slants quite visibly to the left. It is sometimes referred to as slip, knit, pass, or skp.

1 Insert the right needle from front to back into the front (knitwise) of the next stitch on the left needle, and slip it onto the right needle.

2 Knit the next stitch from the left needle.

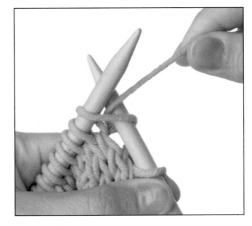

3 Insert the left needle into the front of the slipped stitch, and bring the slipped stitch over the knit stitch and off the needle.

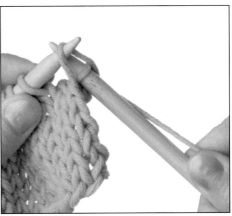

To make your shaping symmetrical, or to shape while maintaining a particular stitch pattern, you sometimes need to decrease two stitches at a time. For example, if you're working seed stitch or single rib, you can keep the stitch pattern correct by knitting or purling 3 stitches together.

KNIT OR PURL 3 TOGETHER

The knit or purl 3 together are the easiest double decreases and are good for decreasing more stitches quickly. The resulting stitch is chunky-looking and slants visibly to the right.

① Insert the right needle into the front of the next 3 stitches (as if to knit) on the left needle.

② Wrap the yarn around the right needle and knit the 3 stitches as 1 stitch.

You have just decreased 2 stitches.

Note: *Work the purl 3 together double decrease in the same manner, only purl the 3 stitches together.*

BASIC DOUBLE DECREASE

The basic double decrease is worked on either side of an axis stitch, and is good for symmetrical shaping.

① Work a slip, slip, knit decrease (see p. 112) over the 2 stitches before the axis stitch.

② Knit the axis stitch.

③ Knit together the next 2 stitches after the axis stitch.

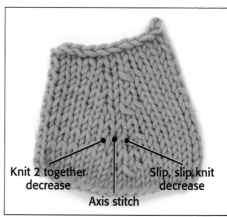

Knit 2 together decrease

Axis stitch

Slip, slip knit decrease

LEFT-SLANTING DOUBLE DECREASE

This double decrease, also called slip 1, knit 2 together, pass slipped stitch over (or sk2p), is good for symmetrical shaping. It looks a bit neater than the basic double decrease, but it does slant visibly to the left on the knit side. You work it on the knit side.

① Slip the next stitch on the left needle knitwise to the right needle.

② Knit the next 2 stitches on the left needle together.

③ Insert the left needle tip into the slipped stitch and lift it up and over the knit 2 together stitch, and off the right needle.

You have now decreased 2 stitches.

CONTINUED ON NEXT PAGE

RIGHT-SLANTING DOUBLE DECREASE

This double decrease slants to the right and is good for symmetrical shaping. What is unusual about it is that a stitch is passed over on the left needle. You work it on the knit side.

1. Slip the next stitch on the left needle knitwise to the right needle.

2. Knit the next stitch, and then pass the slipped stitch over the knit stitch and off the right needle.

   You have now decreased 1 stitch.

3. Slip the decreased knit stitch from the right needle back to the left needle.

4. Insert the right needle into the front of the second stitch on the left needle, and pass it over the decreased knit stitch and off the left needle.

5. Slip the decreased knit stitch from the left needle back to the right needle.

   You have now decreased 2 stitches.

DOUBLE VERTICAL DECREASE

This double decrease results in symmetrical shaping with a raised vertical stitch in the center. You work it over a series of rows on the knit side. Purl side rows are worked without decreases.

1. Insert the right needle into the next 2 stitches on the left needle as if to knit them together and slip them off the left needle and onto the right needle.

2. Knit the next stitch from the left needle.

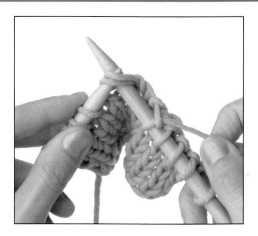

3. Use the left needle to pick up both slipped stitches at the same time, and pass them over the knit stitch and off the right needle.

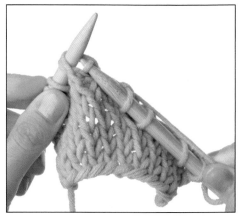

You can decrease stitches to create a right angle for an armhole, or a neck opening by binding off stitches. In general, you don't bind off stitches at the end of a row, unless you're finishing.

AT THE BEGINNING OF A ROW

To shape an armhole or cardigan neck edge, you bind off stitches at the beginning of the row:

1. Work the first 2 stitches. You should now have 2 stitches on the right needle.

2. Insert the left needle into the first stitch worked, and lift it up and over the second stitch.

3. Work 1 stitch.

4. Repeat steps 2–3 until you have bound off the number of stitches indicated in your instructions.

IN THE MIDDLE OF A ROW

To shape a pullover neck or create an inset pocket, you bind off stitches in the middle of the row.

1. Work across the row to 2 stitches before the point where you want the opening to be.

2. Work the next 2 stitches.

3. Insert the left needle into the first of the 2 stitches worked in step 2, and lift it up and over the second stitch.

4. Work 1 stitch.

5. Repeat steps 3–4 until you have bound off the number of stitches indicated in your instructions.

Note: *When working across the following row, you join a second ball of yarn to work the stitches on the far side of the bound-off opening.*

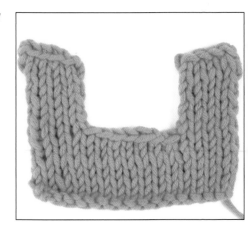

Increase and Decrease Multiple Stitches Across a Row

Some patterns ask you to increase or decrease a certain number of stitches evenly across a row when the knitting needs to quickly become substantially wider or narrower. You should use whichever increase or decrease method is best suited for your stitch pattern.

INCREASING MULTIPLE STITCHES ACROSS 1 ROW

1. To increase stitches evenly across a row, start by adding 1 to the number of stitches that need to be added.

2. Divide the number obtained in step 1 into the number of stitches on your needles to determine the number of stitches to work between increases. (For example, if you have 30 stitches and you are asked to increase 5 stitches evenly, then you knit 5 stitches, increase 1, knit 5, increase 1, and so on.)

3. If the result is not exact, you approximate and work fewer stitches between *some* of the increases, spreading the correct number of increases across the row as evenly as possible.

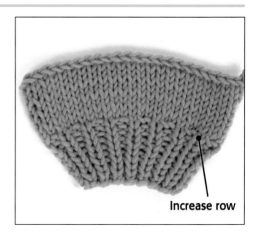

Increase row

DECREASING MULTIPLE STITCHES ACROSS 1 ROW

1. To decrease stitches evenly across a row, divide the number of stitches that you have on your needles by the number that you need to decrease.

2. Subtract 2 from the result to determine the number of stitches to work between decreases. (For example, if you have 30 stitches and you are asked to decrease 10 stitches evenly, then you knit 1 stitch, work the decrease over the next 2 stitches, knit 1 stitch, and so on.)

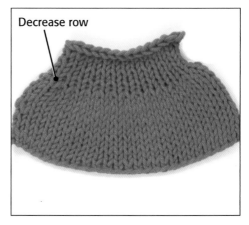

Decrease row

Working a series of partial rows—instead of decreasing or increasing stitches—to create curved or slanted edges, is called *short-rowing*. Short-rowing eliminates the stair steps that occur when binding off stitches over a few rows, and so it's an excellent choice for shaped shoulders, necklines, and sock heels.

SHORT-ROWING ON THE KNIT SIDE

1. Work across the row to the point where the work should be turned. Keeping the working yarn at the back, slip the next stitch purlwise from the left needle to the right needle.

2. Bring the working yarn between the needles to the front, and slip the same stitch that you slipped in step 1 back to the left needle.

3. Bring the working yarn to the back, thereby wrapping the slipped stitch.

4. Turn your work, ready to work the wrong side.

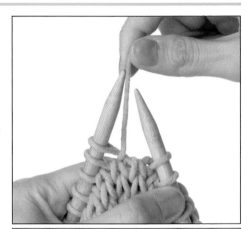

SHORT-ROWING ON THE PURL SIDE

Here's how to continue the short rows on the purl side.

1. On the purl side, work across to the point where the work should be turned. Keep the working yarn at the front, and slip the next stitch purlwise from the left needle to the right needle.

2. Bring the working yarn between the needles to the back, and slip the same stitch that you slipped in step 1 back to the left needle.

3. Bring the working yarn to the front, thereby wrapping the slipped stitch.

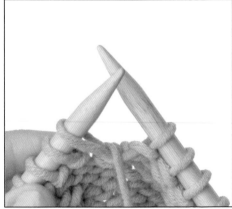

HIDING THE SHORT-ROW WRAPS ON THE KNIT SIDE

After you complete a short row, you hide your wraps to tidy your work. Here's how to do it on the knit side.

1. On the knit side, work to the point where the wrap is.

2. Insert the right needle knitwise under both the wrap and the wrapped stitch.

3. Knit the wrap and the wrapped stitch as 1 stitch.

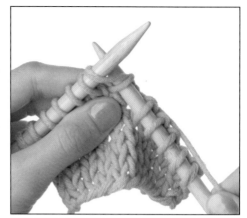

HIDING THE SHORT-ROW WRAPS ON THE PURL SIDE

Here's how to hide the short-row wraps on the purl side.

1. On the purl side, work to the point where the wrap is.

2. Insert the right needle from back to front through the back loop of the wrap. Lift the wrap and place it onto the left needle with the wrapped stitch.

3. Purl the wrap and the wrapped stitch as 1 stitch.

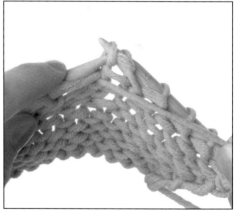

TIP

Three-Needle Bind-off Works for Short-row Shoulders, Too

You can use the three-needle bind-off to join shoulders that have been shaped with short rows. That way, you get the benefit of shaped shoulders *and* the neat and nearly invisible seam formed by the three-needle bind-off. Instead of binding off the shoulder stitches after short-row shaping, simply leave the stitches on a holder, and when both front and back are complete, graft them using the three-needle bind-off. (See p. 42 for instructions.)

chapter 10

Color Knitting

One of the most enjoyable aspects of knitting can be choosing the colors—standing in the yarn shop, holding one ball of yarn next to another to see how they work together. You can use color in your knitting to create beautiful, vibrant designs using several methods: simple horizontal striping; Fair Isle knitting, which involves the stranding of two colors in one row; slip-stitch color knitting, which is a deceptively easy way to create elaborate color patterns; and intarsia knitting, which involves the use of bobbins to create isolated blocks of color. Color choice can play a less important role when you need to showcase a special stitch pattern, or suit a particular style. Take your time when choosing colors, and look to this chapter to learn ways to integrate them into your projects.

One of the many joys of designing handknits is choosing the colors. It's easy to choose one color of yarn; however, choosing colors that work well together can be challenging. Remember that you'll be spending many hours knitting in this scheme, and so you want to choose colors that complement each other *and* that you like—whether they be different shades of blue or high-contrast opposites. Here are a few color concepts to consider when choosing colors.

CHOOSING COLORS THAT WORK WELL TOGETHER

Sometimes it's hard to choose colors that go well together. You may find yourself drawn to the same color combinations over and over again, and decide that you need to go in a new direction; or perhaps the color combination that you would choose is not available in a particular yarn. You can use a 12-part color wheel, as shown, to help you in your choice. To use it, simply choose a starting color. Then aim one of the arrows or points of the triangles or rectangles to the starting color and see what colors the color selector recommends. A color wheel might help you find a color combination that you never would have chosen on your own.

CHOOSING A MONO-CHROMATIC COLOR SCHEME

An easy way to select colors that work well together—and you don't need a color wheel for this—is to choose monochromatic colors. A monochromatic scheme uses variations of the same color, as shown here, in this soothing, quiet combination of blue colors.

CHOOSING AN ANALOGOUS COLOR SCHEME

Another easy option is an analogous color scheme—that is, a scheme made up of three to five adjacent colors on the wheel. The result of this type of combination is generally harmonious and peaceful, as shown here. For example, you may have one color of yarn that you know you want to use, and you want to choose some colors to go with it. You can match your yarn to its corresponding color on the wheel and then choose yarns that match the adjacent colors on either side.

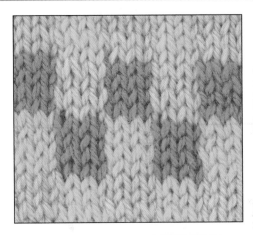

CHOOSING A COMPLEMENTARY COLOR SCHEME

A complementary color scheme is made up of two colors that are opposites on the color wheel. This high-contrast combination is bold and appealing; however, bright opposites placed together sometimes vibrate so much that they're hard to look at. The swatch shown here is knit in violet and yellow; blue and orange are also complements, as are red and green.

CONTINUED ON NEXT PAGE

CHOOSING A TRIADIC COLOR SCHEME

When you choose three colors that are equidistant from one another on the wheel, you have selected a triadic color scheme. There are four triadic color schemes: the primary triad, made up of red, yellow, and blue; the secondary triad, made up of orange, green, and violet; and two tertiary triads, one made up of red-orange, yellow-green, and blue-violet, and the other made up of red-violet, yellow-orange, and blue-green. The primary triadic color scheme shown here conveys a childlike simplicity and can be a little sterile, while secondary and tertiary triadic schemes are rich, subtle, and complex.

CHOOSING A SPLIT COMPLEMENTARY COLOR SCHEME

This swatch is an example of a split complementary color scheme. This type of color scheme is made up of three colors: a starting color and the two colors on either side of its complement. For example, if you had violet yarn and wanted to try a split complementary color combination, you would choose a ball of yellowish green and a ball of orange to go with it, because those are the two colors on either side of yellow—violet's complement.

CHOOSING A TETRADIC COLOR SCHEME

Things become complicated when you work with a tetradic color scheme. Usually a daring color statement, a tetradic color scheme is made up of two sets of complementary colors. For example, a tetradic color scheme might be made up of red, green, orange, and blue because red and green are complements, as are orange and blue. Experiment with various amounts of each of these colors, as four competing opposites can be difficult to look at all at once.

Note: *The swatch shown here is made up of more orange-red than the other colors.*

EXPERIMENTING WITH COLOR

After you've pored over the color wheel, you can knit up test swatches in different color combinations to see how they actually work. This swatch uses the same stitch pattern in three assorted combinations. It's remarkable how dissimilar the same design can look in different color combinations.

Make Horizontal Stripes

Working horizontal stripes is one of the easiest ways to combine more than one color in your knitting. If you know how to knit, purl, and change to a new ball of yarn, then you can knit horizontal stripes. Stripe patterns are easiest to knit if you use an even number of rows for each stripe. This way, changing colors always occurs at the same edge, enabling you to carry the yarn up the side of your work, and ultimately saving you the trouble of weaving in a lot of ends later.

IN STOCKINETTE STITCH

1 To make a stripe in a contrast color, work as many rows as you want the first stripe to be. At the beginning of the next row, drop the old yarn and knit or purl across the row in the new yarn, depending on which side you are on.

2 Carry the yarns up the side by twisting the first yarn around the second yarn at the edge of every other row. (If the stripes are only two rows each, this is not necessary; the yarns will be carried up sufficiently on their own.)

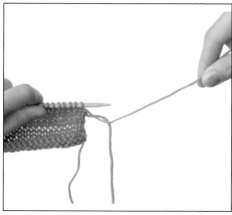

IN RIBBING

Work as many rows as you want the first stripe to be, ending with a wrong-side row. At the beginning of the next row, drop the old yarn and knit all stitches in the new color. Work the subsequent rows in the ribbing pattern as established, until it is time to change colors again. Alternatively, if you're working ribbing stripes for an odd number of rows, and you are switching colors on the wrong side, then purl the first row of the new color.

Note: Knitting on the right side or purling on the wrong side the first row of a new color ensures that the color break will be smooth on the right side.

IN GARTER STITCH

If you're knitting a scarf or other two-sided project, color bumps could become part of the design. However, if you want to knit garter stitch stripes without the broken lines, you need to change colors on the same side every time—this will be the right side—and you need to work stripes over even numbers of rows only. The swatch here shows garter stitch stripes made up of even numbers of rows.

TIP

Corrugated Ribbing: Another Way to Work Stripes in Ribbing

You can work ribbing in two colors in another way: in corrugated ribbing using vertical stripes. You see corrugated ribbing on the cuffs and hems of a lot of Scandinavian sweaters. It's a lively accent, and it creates a firm edging that looks like ribbing, but is not as stretchy. You work it by knitting the knit stitches of the rib in one color, and purling the purl stitches of the rib in a second color. For example, if you're working a knit 2, purl 2 rib, you would knit 2 in the first color, purl 2 in the second color, knit 2 in the first color, and so on. On the wrong side, you purl the stitches in the first color, and knit the stitches in the second color.

Fair Isle knitting involves working with two colors across a row, carrying both yarns across the back. The challenge in Fair Isle knitting is maintaining tension: If the yarns stranded along the back are too tight, then your knitting will pucker and have no elasticity; if they are too loose, then your stitches will look uneven.

There are a couple of ways to approach Fair Isle knitting. When the intervals between color changes are no more than 4 stitches, you can do one-handed or two-handed stranding.

ONE-HANDED STRANDING ON THE KNIT SIDE

① Work to the point in the row where you need to change colors. Let go of yarn A, pick up yarn B and bring it above and over yarn A, and knit the correct number of stitches in yarn B.

Note: To avoid puckering, you need to keep the stitches on the right needle spread apart so that you can strand a sufficient length of the non-working yarn across the back.

② Work to the point in the row where you need to change colors again. Let go of yarn B, pick up yarn A and bring it underneath yarn B, and knit until the next color shift.

③ Repeat steps 1–2, taking care to keep yarn A underneath yarn B when changing colors.

Note: Always carry both yarns to the end of the row because the color pattern may call for the other color to begin the next row.

ONE-HANDED STRANDING ON THE PURL SIDE

① Work to the point in the row where you need to change colors. Let go of yarn A, pick up yarn B and bring it above and over yarn A, and purl the correct number of stitches in yarn B.

② When you reach the point in the row where you need to change colors again, let go of yarn B, pick up yarn A and bring it underneath yarn B, and purl until the next color shift.

③ Repeat steps 1–2, taking care to keep yarn A underneath yarn B when changing colors.

Note: *Always carry both yarns to the end of the row because the color pattern may call for the other color to begin the next row.*

CONTINUED ON NEXT PAGE

TIP

Yarn in tangles?

It's easy for yarns to tangle when you're knitting with more than one. Keeping the same yarn above and the same yarn below when changing colors helps; also, do not twist yarns when you turn your knitting to switch from the right side to the wrong side, and vice versa. You can also try keeping each yarn in its own zipper seal bag; cut a little corner off the bottom for the strand to come out, and zip the ball into the bag. This is more portable than using plastic containers, boxes, or lidded drinking cups, which also work at keeping the yarns from rolling around and getting tangled. Either way, if the yarns do snarl up, it's easy to rearrange the bags or containers to correct the problem.

TWO-HANDED STRANDING ON THE KNIT SIDE

1. Hold yarn A in your right hand, English style, and yarn B in your left hand, Continental style.

2. Knit with yarn A in your right hand, holding it above yarn B, to the point in the row where you need to change colors.

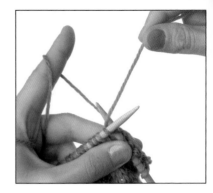

3. Knit with your left hand using yarn B, which should automatically come from underneath yarn A.

4. Repeat steps 1–3.

   Note: Always carry both yarns to the end of the row because the color pattern may call for the other color to begin the next row.

TIP

Fixing Uneven Fair Isle Stitches
Often Fair Isle knitting comes out looking a little uneven, or slightly puckered. You can easily neaten and smooth the rough surface by giving your Fair Isle knitting a quick, light steam with an iron. Do not press down on the knitting; lightly run the iron, steam on, over the surface, and watch the imperfections disappear.

TWO-HANDED STRANDING ON THE PURL SIDE

1. Hold yarn A in your right hand, English style, and yarn B in your left hand, Continental style.

2. Purl with yarn A in your right hand, holding it above yarn B, to the point in the row where you need to change colors.

3. Purl with your left hand using yarn B, which should automatically come from underneath yarn A.

4. Repeat steps 1–3.

   Note: Always carry both yarns to the end of the row because the color pattern may call for the other color to begin the next row.

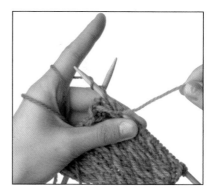

TIP

Combining Fair Isle and One-Color Knitting

You might have noticed that you don't get the same gauge when knitting Fair Isle patterns as you do using the same yarn on the same-size needles in one-color stockinette stitch. This can be tricky when you're working a garment that is a combination of the two. Often the row gauge in Fair Isle knitting is close to or equal to the stitch gauge because Fair Isle stitches have a more square appearance. It is not uncommon for the stitch gauge to be slightly compressed. If you're working on a fabric that combines large blocks of non-Fair Isle with segments of Fair Isle, try working the Fair Isle section using needles one size larger. Work up a gauge sample that combines the stitches to see if this works for you.

Weave Yarns in Fair Isle Knitting

When your color pattern has more than 4 stitches between color changes or more than two colors per row, you carry the non-working yarn along the back by weaving it in and out of the backs of every few stitches made in the working yarn. How you weave depends on whether you're knitting or purling, as well as which hand is holding the working yarn and which is holding the weaving yarn.

WEAVING IN, KNIT SIDE: WORKING YARN RIGHT, WEAVING YARN LEFT

1. Holding yarn A (the working yarn) in your right hand, English style, and yarn B (the yarn that will be woven in back) in your left hand, Continental style, insert the right needle into the next stitch on the left needle. Move your finger to bring yarn B from back to front, and lay it against the tip of the right needle. Wrap yarn A as usual to prepare to knit the stitch.

2. Knit the stitch.

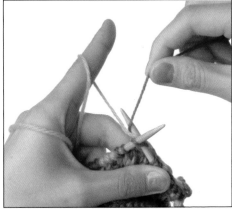

3. Move your finger to bring yarn B away from the needles as usual. When you knit the next stitch, yarn B gets caught under the horizontal bar between this new stitch and the last stitch.

WEAVING IN, KNIT SIDE: WORKING YARN LEFT, WEAVING YARN RIGHT

1 Holding yarn A (the weaving yarn) in your right hand, English style, and yarn B (the working yarn) in your left hand, Continental style, insert the right needle into the next stitch on the left needle. Wrap yarn A around the right needle as you would to knit; then wrap yarn B around the right needle as you would to knit.

2 Bring yarn A back off the right needle to where it came from, leaving yarn B wrapped around the right needle, ready to be knit.

3 Knit the stitch.

CONTINUED ON NEXT PAGE

One-Handed Stranded Knitting

If two-handed stranding is not for you, there are a couple of one-handed options that are more efficient than dropping the yarns each time you change colors. You can hold one yarn looped around your index finger, and another yarn looped around your middle finger. Or you can buy a *yarn guide ring* to wear on your index finger. It has several holes at the top that guide and separate the different strands of yarn while you work your color knitting.

WEAVING IN, PURL SIDE: WORKING YARN RIGHT, WEAVING YARN LEFT

① Holding yarn A (the working yarn) in your right hand, English style, and yarn B (the yarn that will be woven in back) in your left hand, Continental style, insert the right needle into the next stitch as if to purl. Move your finger to bring yarn B from front to back, and lay it against the tip of the right needle. Wrap yarn A as usual to prepare to purl the stitch.

② Purl the stitch.

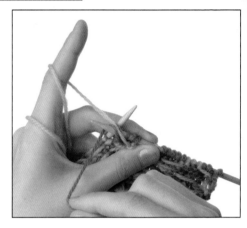

③ Before purling the next stitch, bring yarn B down and away from the needles; wrap yarn A as usual and then purl the stitch.

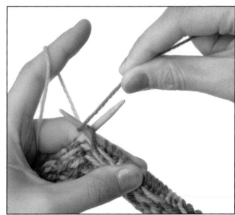

WEAVING IN, PURL SIDE: WORKING YARN LEFT, WEAVING YARN RIGHT

1. Holding yarn A (the weaving yarn) in your right hand, English style, and yarn B (the working yarn) in your left hand, Continental style, insert the right needle into the next stitch as if to purl. Bring yarn A under the right needle from front to back; then lay yarn B over the tip of the right needle from front to back.

2. Bring yarn A back to the front—to where it came from (it will be hooked around yarn B)—and then draw yarn B through to purl the stitch.

3. Hold yarn A down away from the needles, and purl another stitch using yarn B.

Slip-Stitch Color Knitting

Slip-stitch color knitting, also known as *mosaic* or *colorship knitting*, is another way to work with two colors at the same time, without stranding or using bobbins. You don't even have to change colors mid-row. You work one color at a time in each row, using the same color over two consecutive rows, and slipping the stitches purlwise that will be worked in the second color on the following two rows. You can work slip-stitch knitting in stockinette stitch, or in garter stitch, following either a chart or row-by-row instructions.

READING A SLIP-STITCH COLOR CHART

Some slip-stitch patterns are worked from charts; others are written out with indications of how many stitches to knit or purl, and how many stitches to slip. Right-side rows are read right to left, and wrong-side rows are read left to right. Unlike other stitch pattern charts, rows are numbered on both the right and the left sides of the chart—odd numbers on the right, even numbers on the left—and *every* row is labeled with an odd and even number. For example, the first row is labeled 1 on the right, and 2 on the left; the second row is labeled 3 on the right, and 4 on the left. This is because the second pattern row, the wrong-side row, is worked the same as the right-side row preceding it: The same stitches that are knit on the right side are worked on the wrong side, and the same stitches that are slipped on the right side, are slipped on the wrong side. Most charts also have a color key running alongside the chart to show the working color for each row.

The knit sample that is shown here corresponds to the chart above.

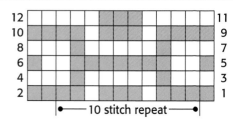

WORKING SLIP-STITCH KNITTING

1 Cast on in the color that will be the working yarn for the first 2 rows. For the first row (a right-side row), knit the stitches, following the chart from left to right, in the working color, and slip the stitches in the second color purlwise, holding the working yarn at the back.

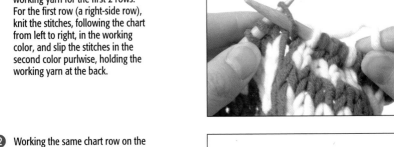

2 Working the same chart row on the wrong side, reading from left to right, purl all of the stitches in the working color, and slip the stitches in the second color purlwise, while holding the working yarn at the front.

Note: If you are working your slip-stitch pattern in garter stitch, knit the stitches in the working color for step 2.

TIP

Avoiding the Pucker in Slip-Stitch Knitting

Some slip-stitch color patterns call for slipping more than 3 stitches consecutively, which can result in a tight and puckered fabric. If your chart indicates slipping 5 or more stitches in a row, then you'll have to catch the working yarn in the middle of the span of slipped stitches to prevent this tightness. To do this, you bring the working yarn to the front on the knit side, and to the back on the purl side, and then slip the next stitch in the group. The drawback to this technique is that you get a little nub of the working color in the middle of your slipped section.

Intarsia, or *bobbin*, knitting is another form of color knitting. Unlike Fair Isle—where colors are worked and carried across rows in a repetitive pattern—with intarsia you can scatter isolated blocks of color over your knitting, or put one large motif on a background of another color. You knit each motif using a separate ball or bobbin of yarn. When changing colors, you twist yarns together on the wrong side to avoid leaving holes on the right side.

1 On the right side, knit to the place where the intarsia motif is to begin, drop the main color yarn, and get ready to knit with the contrast color yarn.

Note: You might want to tie the new yarn to the old yarn before knitting the first stitch of the new color. This helps to maintain even tension. You can untie it and secure the loose end later. Just be sure to leave at least a 6-inch tail on the new yarn.

2 Knit the number of stitches in the contrast color as indicated by your pattern.

3 Drop the contrast color and begin knitting from a new bobbin of your main color. Work to the end of the right-side row.

4 On the wrong side, purl using the main color until you reach the point where the color change should occur.

5 Drop the main color, twist the yarns together by bringing the contrast color up from underneath the main color, and purl as many stitches in the contrast color as the pattern requires.

6 Drop the contrast color, twist the yarns together by picking up the main color from underneath the contrast color, and purl the next stitch. Continue as the pattern directs.

TIP

Easy Three- (or More) Color Intarsia

Unlike the intarsia sample here, many intarsia motifs are made up of more than one color. Managing three or more colors with bobbin knitting can be messy and rather unpleasant. If your motif has more than one color, but the second or third color appears as only a few stitches here and there, then you can cheat and work that part of the motif as a duplicate stitch (see p. 204). The resulting color work will be neater, particularly if you are new to intarsia.

chapter 11

Finishing Techniques

After you complete the knitting stage of a project, it is time to move on to finishing. Finishing consists of weaving in the loose ends that hang off your knitting, blocking your knit pieces to the correct measurements, and putting the pieces together by sewing seams. Although most knitters prefer knitting to finishing, mastering the finishing techniques in this chapter will ensure that you are happy with your completed projects.

Weave in Ends

Weaving in ends, either horizontally across the work or vertically up the side, is what you do to get rid of all of the loose yarns that are dangling from your knitting. To make managing yarn ends easier, be sure to leave at least a 6-inch tail when casting on, binding off, joining new yarn, or cutting an end. You need at least that length to properly weave in an end. If you leave your ends too short, they can work their way loose, and your knitting can unravel.

WEAVE IN ENDS UP THE SIDE

1 Thread a tail of yarn through a tapestry needle that is appropriate for the thickness of your yarn.

2 With the wrong side facing, bring the tapestry needle in and out from back to front, up the side of the knitting.

3 After you have woven in the end a few inches, cut it close to the work, taking great care not to cut your knitting.

TIP

Yarn Ends Too Short?
If you find your yarn ends are too short to weave in with a tapestry needle, you can use a crochet hook to pull the end of the yarn through the backs of as many stitches as possible.

WEAVE IN ENDS ACROSS THE BACK

1. Thread the tail of yarn through the tapestry needle.

2. With the wrong side facing, weave the tapestry needle in and out of the backs of the stitches in a straight, diagonal line for 2–3 inches.

3. Weave the tapestry needle in and out of the backs of the stitches in the opposite direction, right next to the first diagonal line, for about 1 inch.

4. Cut the yarn end close to the work, taking great care not to cut your knitting.

   Note: You can lightly stretch your knitting to pull the yarn end further into the work to conceal it.

TIP

Weaving in Ends on Two-Sided Knitting

You can weave in ends invisibly into stitch patterns that are reversible, like garter stitch, seed stitch, and certain ribbings. One option is to work the end in duplicate stitch (see p. 204) on either side. Another way is to weave the end over and under, imitating and following the lines of the stitches.

Block Your Knitting

Steam blocking and wet blocking are wonderful fixers of imperfections. Blocking consists of moistening knitted pieces, shaping them with pins, and allowing them to dry so that they hold the proper shape in the correct measurements.

Always use rustproof pins and check your yarn's care instructions to ensure that applying moisture, heat, or steam is safe.

STEAM BLOCKING

1. Lay a knitted piece flat on a padded surface. Pin only at enough points to hold the piece straight for the time being.

2. Measure the knitted piece to ensure that it has the same dimensions that the pattern specifies. Adjust the pins, as needed, to match the measurements and make the piece even.

   Note: Do not stretch and pin ribbing at cuffs and hems unless the pattern indicates to do so. After ribbing is stretched and blocked, it is no longer elastic.

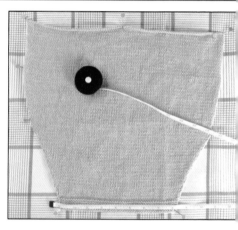

3. When the measurements are correct, pin the piece all around.

4. Cover the piece with a light cloth. (You can dampen the cloth with a spray bottle, if desired.) Slowly and gently, run the iron over the entire piece, excluding ribbing, and be sure not to press or distort the knitting.

5. Allow the piece to dry before removing the pins.

6. Repeat steps 1–5 for all pieces of your project. Be sure that all of the pieces are completely dry before sewing the seams.

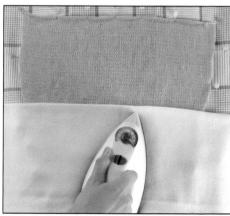

WET BLOCKING

1. Lay a knitted piece flat on a padded surface. Pin only at enough points to hold the piece straight for the time being.

2. Measure the knitted piece to ensure that it has the same dimensions that the pattern specifies. Adjust the pins as needed, to match the measurements and make the piece even.

   Note: Do not stretch and pin ribbing at cuffs and hems unless the pattern indicates to do so. After ribbing is stretched and blocked, it is no longer elastic.

3. When the measurements are correct, pin the piece all around.

4. Wet the piece thoroughly with a spray bottle.

5. Allow the piece to dry before removing the pins.

6. Repeat steps 1–5 for all pieces of your project. Be sure that all of the pieces are completely dry before sewing the seams.

TIP

Do Not Put the Iron Away Yet

If you used a steamer or steam iron to do your blocking, don't put it away just yet. After you have sewn your seams, knit on button bands and collars, and sewn on pockets, you will want to neaten everything up with a quick steam. Run the iron, steam on, very lightly over your newly sewn seams to tidy them and reduce bulk. Do the same for collars, button bands, and pockets.

There are numerous ways to sew seams. The invisible horizontal seam is an excellent choice for bound-off shoulder seams and other horizontal edges, while the invisible vertical seam works well for sweater sides and other vertical edges. The backstitch seam is a good catchall method but is bulkier than the other seams covered here. You can also crochet a seam together by using the same yarn that you used to knit your project, or yarn that is slightly thinner for less bulk.

INVISIBLE VERTICAL SEAM

① Thread a tapestry needle with a long enough strand of yarn to sew the seam and leave a 6-inch tail.

② To join the pieces: With the right sides up, line up the vertical edges exactly. Sew 1 stitch at the base of the seam, and insert the needle from back to front through the space between the first and second stitches on the lower-right corner of the left piece. Pull the yarn through until only about 6 inches remain. Insert the needle from front to back between the first and second stitches in the lower-left corner of the right piece; bring the needle back through the same spot on the left piece again. Pull the yarn through snugly.

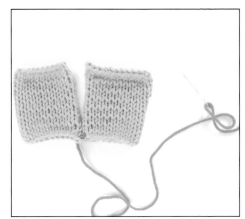

Now you are ready to work the invisible vertical seam.

③ Find the horizontal bar of yarn between the first and second stitches. Insert the needle under the horizontal bar, between the first and second stitches, 1 stitch up from the joining stitch, on the right piece. Pull the yarn through.

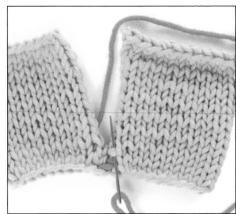

④ Insert the needle under the horizontal bar between the first and second stitches, 1 stitch up from the joining stitch, on the left piece. Pull the yarn through.

⑤ Insert the needle under the next horizontal bar up on the right side and then under the corresponding bar on the left side. Continue in this manner, alternating from side to side, to the end of the seam. Pull the yarn ends to close the seam.

⑥ Weave in the loose ends.

Note: *A contrast color yarn was used here to sew the seam for illustrative purposes. Be sure to sew your seams with the yarn that you used to knit the pieces for your seams.*

CONTINUED ON NEXT PAGE

TIP

Invisible Seams for 1 x 1 Ribbing

You can make your ribbing seams look invisible. For this to work with 1 x 1 ribbing, you need an odd number of stitches. Begin and end each right-side row of the pieces to be joined with a knit stitch. Then, when it is time to sew the seams, use the invisible vertical method, but pick up the bars a *half* stitch in from the edge. The join will look like 1 knit stitch.

INVISIBLE VERTICAL SEAM FOR GARTER STITCH AND REVERSE STOCKINETTE STITCH

① Thread a tapestry needle with a long enough strand of yarn to sew the seam and leave a 6-inch tail.

② To join the pieces: With the right sides up, line up the vertical edges exactly. Sew 1 stitch at the base of the seam and insert the needle from back to front through the space between the first and second stitches on the lower-left corner of the right piece. Pull the yarn through until about 6 inches of yarn remain. Insert the needle from front to back between the first and second stitches in the lower-right corner of the left piece; bring the needle back through the same spot on the right piece again. Pull the yarn through snugly.

③ Insert the tapestry needle up into the bottom loop (it looks like a smile) of the first stitch on the right piece and pull the yarn through, but not too tightly.

④ Insert the tapestry needle up into the top loop (it looks like a frown) of the corresponding stitch on the left piece, and pull the yarn through.

⑤ Continue in this manner, alternating from side to side, pulling yarn snugly every few stitches to tighten it, until the seam is sewn.

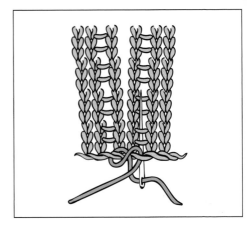

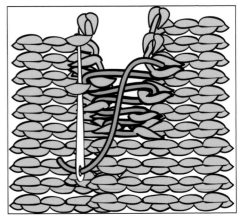

INVISIBLE HORIZONTAL SEAM

1. Thread a tapestry needle with a long enough strand of yarn to sew the seam and leave a 6-inch tail.

2. With right sides up, line up the bound-off edges exactly. Insert the needle from back to front through the middle of the first stitch of the lower piece, leaving a 6-inch tail.

3. Use the needle to pick up the two loops (the V) of the corresponding stitch on the upper piece. Pull the yarn through.

4. Bring the needle across the seam to the next stitch on the lower piece, and use it to pick up the loops (the upside-down V), threading it through all the way.

5. Repeat steps 3–4 across the seam, pulling the yarn tightly—but not too tightly, or it will pucker—every couple of stitches to neaten it.

6. Weave in the loose ends.

   Note: *A contrast color yarn was used here to sew the seam for illustrative purposes. Be sure to sew your seams with the yarn that you used to knit the pieces for your seams.*

CONTINUED ON NEXT PAGE

TIP

Neater Edges Make Neater Seams

Sometimes side edges, or vertical edges, can be loose and messy. When you join these edges, the messy look can carry over to the seam. You can avoid sloppy edges by slipping the first stitch of every row. The result will be nice, neat edges that are easy to join.

INVISIBLE VERTICAL-TO-HORIZONTAL SEAM

1 Thread a tapestry needle with a long enough strand of yarn to sew the seam and leave a 6-inch tail.

2 With the right sides up, line up the bound-off edge and the side edge, with the bound-off edge as the lower piece and the side edge as the upper piece, as shown.

3 Insert the needle from back to front through the V of the first stitch on the right edge of the lower piece, just below the bound-off edge. Pull the yarn through until about 6 inches remain.

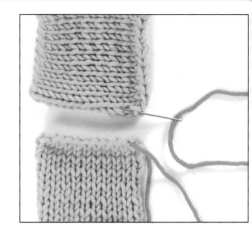

4 Insert the needle on the other side of the join—directly across from the same point on the lower piece—under one of the bars between the first and second stitches on the upper piece. Pull the yarn through.

Note: Because you are matching rows to stitches in this join and there are usually more rows per inch than stitches, you need to pick up two of the bars on the horizontal piece every other stitch or so to keep the seam even.

5 Bring the yarn across the join and pick up the loops that make the point of the upside-down V of the next stitch on the lower piece, just below the bound-off edge. Pull the yarn through, trying to imitate the size of each stitch in the knitted piece.

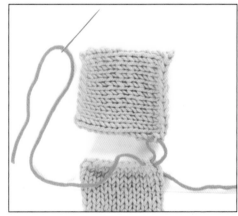

6 Continue alternating back and forth between the upper and lower pieces until you finish the seam.

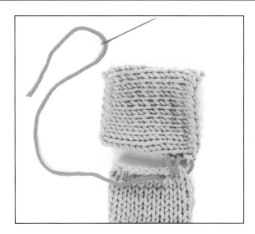

7 Gently pull the yarn ends to close the seam.

8 Weave in the loose ends.

Note: *A contrast color yarn was used here to sew the seam for illustrative purposes. Be sure to sew your seams with the yarn that you used to knit the pieces for your seams.*

CONTINUED ON NEXT PAGE

TIP

Quick Tip: Even Seams

Joining long seams can be tricky: You are sewing away, and suddenly you reach the end and the edges don't line up. You can avoid uneven or puckered seams by tacking the base of the seam with a quick stitch, and then tacking the end-point of the seam together. That way, you ensure that you are working the seam evenly from start to finish.

BACKSTITCH SEAM

1. Thread a tapestry needle with a long enough strand of yarn to sew the seam and leave a 6-inch tail.

2. Place the pieces together, with the right sides facing each other and the seam edge lined up. Secure the edge stitches by bringing the needle through both thicknesses from back to front at the right edge, 1 stitch down from the bound-off stitches, or 1 stitch in from the edge stitches. Do this twice and pull the yarn through.

3. Insert the needle through both thicknesses, from back to front, about 2 stitches to the left, and bring the yarn through.

4. Insert the needle from front to back, about 1 stitch in to the right, and pull the yarn through.

5. Now bring the needle ahead 2 stitches to the left and insert it from back to front.

6. Repeat steps 4–5 across the seam until you reach the end, taking care to insert the needle at the same depth each time.

7. Weave in the loose ends.

   Note: A contrast color yarn was used here to sew the seam for illustrative purposes. Be sure to sew your seams with the yarn that you used to knit the pieces for your seams.

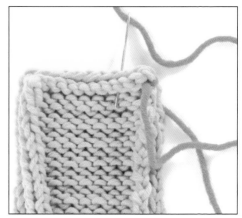

CROCHETED SEAM

1. Choose a crochet hook that is the same size as the needles used to knit your project, and the same yarn, or yarn that is slightly thinner and matches your yarn.

2. Place the pieces together, with the right sides facing each other and the seam edge lined up.

3. Insert the hook through both thicknesses from front to back at the right edge, 1 stitch down from the bound-off stitches, or 1 stitch in from the edge stitches.

4. Wrap yarn over the hook and draw a loop through both thicknesses from back to front.

5. Insert the hook through both thicknesses again, about 1 stitch to the left; wrap yarn over the hook and draw a loop through both thicknesses from back to front, bringing this second loop through the first loop on the hook.

   You should now have 1 loop on the hook.

6. Repeat step 5 across the seam; do not work too tightly or the seam will have no elasticity.

TIP

Seaming with Bulky Yarns and Novelty Yarns

When seaming knits made from highly textured novelty yarns, use a smooth yarn that matches your novelty yarn, and that requires similar care. If you knit your project using a bulky or super-bulky yarn, you may find that sewing seams with the same yarn adds too much bulk. Try sewing seams with a thinner, though similar, matching yarn.

Grafting—which is a good choice for unshaped shoulders, toes of socks, and mitten tips—involves joining an open row of stitches to another open row of stitches or to another edge. The stitches are joined while they're still on the knitting needle, and the final result looks like a row of stockinette stitch. You can graft seams using the three-needle bind-off, already covered in Chapter 4, on p. 42; or you can graft using the Kitchener stitch.

KITCHENER STITCH

1. Have the two sets of stitches that are to be joined, each on a knitting needle as shown.

2. Using yarn that matches your knitting, thread a tapestry needle with a strand that is roughly twice the length of the seam.

3. Lay both pieces of knitting on a table, with the wrong sides down and the needles running parallel to each other, with the tips facing to the right.

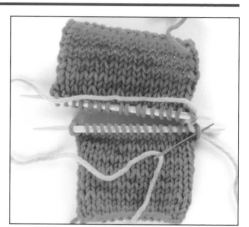

4. Insert the tapestry needle into the first stitch on the lower needle as if to purl; pull the yarn through until only about 6 inches remain. Leave the stitch on the needle.

5. Insert the tapestry needle into the first stitch on the upper needle as if to knit, and pull the yarn through snugly, leaving the stitch on the needle.

6. Insert the tapestry needle into the first stitch on the lower needle again, this time as if to knit; then slip this stitch off the needle.

7. Insert the tapestry needle into the next stitch on the lower needle as if to purl. Leave the stitch on the needle.

8. Insert the tapestry needle into the first stitch on the upper needle again, this time as if to purl; then slip this stitch off the needle.

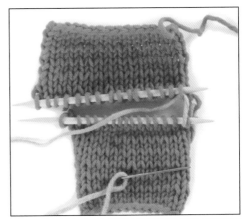

9. Insert the tapestry needle into the next stitch on the upper needle as if to knit. Leave the stitch on the needle.

10. Repeat steps 6–9 until all of the stitches have been completed. Remember: On the lower needle, the first insertion is as if to purl, the second insertion is as if to knit, and then the stitch comes off; on the upper needle, the first insertion is as if to knit, the second insertion is as if to purl, and then the stitch comes off.

Note: A contrast color yarn was used here to graft the seam for illustrative purposes. Be sure to graft your seams with the yarn that you used to knit the pieces for your seams.

TIP

Decorative Three-Needle Bind-Off

You can use the three-needle bind-off (see p. 42) to graft seams if the Kitchener stitch is too complicated to follow. In general, you work the three-needle bind-off with the right sides facing each other, so that the seam is on the wrong side. Three-needle bind-off is such a tidy seam that you can use it with the wrong sides facing, so that the seam is on the right side, as a decorative accent. The result is a raised ridge along the seam.

Assemble a Sweater

You can use one or more of the seam techniques on the previous pages to sew a sweater together. However, before you start joining the pieces, take a few minutes to read about the order of assembly and what seaming technique is best for each part.

ORDER OF ASSEMBLY

Generally, sweaters that are knit flat in pieces are joined first at the shoulders. Then the sleeves are attached. Finally, the side and underarm seams are sewn. You use long straight pins to pin pieces together before seaming. Neaten up the seams by lightly steaming them with an iron after sewing them.

WHICH SEAM FOR WHICH PART?

Sometimes knitting instructions specify the best seaming technique for a given join. If no specific technique is indicated, you can always safely use the backstitch seam for the shoulders, whether they are shaped or not. If the shoulders are not shaped, you can try using the invisible horizontal seam or the three-needle bind-off. Use the table below to make the right choice.

Type of Seam	Use It to Join	Examples
Invisible horizontal seam	Two horizontal edges	Bound-off shoulder seams
Backstitch seam	All edges	Shaped shoulders, side seams, add-on collars
Invisible vertical seam	Two vertical edges	Sweater sides and under-arm seams
Invisible vertical-to-horizontal seam	A bound-off edge to a side edge	Joining a sleeve cap to an armhole
Grafted seam	Two horizontal edges	Unshaped shoulders, toes of socks, mitten tips

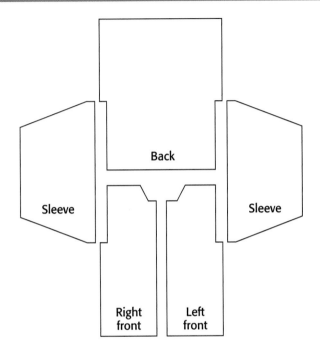

Back

Sleeve

Sleeve

Right
front

Left
front

CONTINUED ON NEXT PAGE

ATTACHING SLEEVES

There are many different ways to shape armholes and sleeve caps. The type of armhole shaping always determines the sleeve cap shaping. After blocking all pieces, working the edging on the neck, and joining and pressing shoulder seams, you can attach the sleeves. How you prepare to attach your sleeve depends on which seam you use. For a perfect seam, the invisible vertical-to-horizontal method is best. If that does not work with your shaping or stitch pattern, you can use the backstitch seam. For either approach, you need to find the center of the sleeve cap by folding the sleeve in half lengthwise. Then mark the center with a safety pin. If you are working the invisible seam, follow the instructions on p. 148. If you are using the backstitch seam, then you need to do some more pinning: After pinning the center of the sleeve cap to the shoulder seam, with the right sides facing each other, pin the rest of the sleeve cap to the armhole, lining up the sleeve cap shaping with the corresponding armhole shaping. Sew the sleeve in place using the backstitch seam, starting at the shoulder seam and working down to one arm-hole edge. Repeat for the other half.

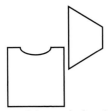

Straight armhole with
straight sleeve cap

Shaped armhole with
rounded set-in sleeve
cap

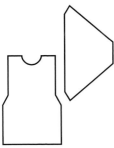

Angular armhole shaping
with angular sleeve cap

Raglan armhole with
raglan sleeve

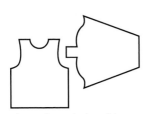
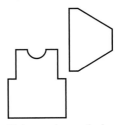

Shaped armhole with
set-in saddle-shoulder
sleeve

Right-angle armhole
with set-in sleeve

Finishing Details

Sometimes the finishing phase of a hand-knit sweater can take almost as long as the knitting phase. However, because you have spent many hours knitting your project, you should spend a few more hours on finishing it to show it off in the best possible light. Besides blocking and seaming pieces together, there are also many finishing details that your project may need, such as buttonholes, collars, hems, and pockets.

Picking up stitches is what you do to add button bands, neckbands, collars, or decorative borders to the already finished edges of your knitting. After you pick up stitches along an edge, you use them to knit the part that you want to add—without having to sew the piece on. You can also pick up stitches at an armhole edge and knit a sleeve from the top down.

HOW TO PICK UP STITCHES ALONG A BOUND-OFF EDGE

1 Start at the top-right corner, with the right side facing, and insert the needle into the center of the V of the first stitch, just below the bound-off row.

2 Wrap the working yarn around the needle as you would to knit, holding a 6-inch tail.

3 Bring the loop of the working yarn to the front, as you would to knit.

You have now picked up your first stitch.

4 Repeat steps 1–3 across the edge, working from right to left, for each stitch.

Note: When you are done picking up stitches and are ready to begin knitting, be sure to switch back to your working needles.

HOW TO PICK UP STITCHES ALONG A VERTICAL EDGE

① Turn your work so that the vertical rows run horizontally and the right side is facing.

② Starting at the right corner of the pick-up edge, insert the right needle from front to back into the space between the first and second stitches, as shown. Wrap the working yarn around the right needle as you would to knit, holding a 6-inch tail.

③ Bring the loop of working yarn to the front, as you would to knit.

You have now picked up your first stitch.

④ Repeat steps 1–3 across the edge, working from right to left, skipping a row every few stitches.

Note: Because there are more rows per inch than stitches, you do not need to insert the needle between every stitch along a vertical edge. Doing so results in an edge that looks stretched out; skipping a row every few pick-up stitches makes up for the difference.

CONTINUED ON NEXT PAGE

TIP

Calculating How Many Stitches to Pick Up

It's easy to know how many stitches to pick up along a bound-off edge, such as a pocket top: You simply pick up 1 stitch in each stitch across the row. Because row height is less than stitch width, picking up stitches along a vertical edge is less straightforward. A good rule to remember when picking up stitches along a vertical edge is to pick up approximately 3 stitches for every 4 rows.

HOW TO PICK UP STITCHES ALONG A CURVED EDGE

1 Starting at the top-right corner, with the right side facing, insert the needle into the center of the V of the first stitch, just below the bound-off edge of the shaping.

2 Wrap the working yarn around the needle, as you would to knit, holding a 6-inch tail.

3 Pick up all of the stitches on the horizontal section of the shaping until you get to the vertical section.

4 Continue picking up stitches as you would for a vertical edge, skipping a row every few stitches, if necessary. Be sure not to insert the needle into any large holes that are caused by the shaping, as doing so will result in a hole in your picked-up edge.

HOW TO PICK UP STITCHES EVENLY

1 Place pins, spaced evenly apart, along the edge where the stitches are to be picked up.

Note: Instead of using pins, you can tie bits of yarn as markers at even intervals along the edge.

2 Calculate how many stitches should be picked up between markers by dividing the total number of stitches to be picked up by the number of spaces between pins.

3 Pick up the appropriate number of stitches between each pair of markers.

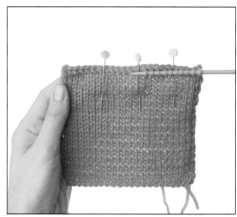

TIP

Closing the Gaps

Sometimes you get little gaps or holes when picking up stitches around corners, as for a shaped neck, mitten or glove thumb, or sock gusset. You can close up these gaps somewhat by picking up an extra stitch at the problem spot. Just be sure to knit the extra stitch together with its neighbor on the next row or round to get back to the correct stitch count.

Button Bands, Neckbands, Plackets, and Collars

Some sweater patterns call for bands and collars that are knit as separate pieces and sewn on at the end. Others indicate that you knit the band or collar directly onto the garment by picking up stitches. Either way, it is a good idea to acquaint yourself with the various parts of a sweater.

NECKBANDS AND BUTTON BANDS

Neckbands are frequently worked on smaller needles in ribbing, seed stitch, or garter stitch. Neck shaping alone can have an unfinished look, and so it is usually desirable to attach or knit on a neckband. There are many varieties of neckbands— crewneck, V neck, and square neck, to name a few.

Some cardigans are finished with strips of knitting along the vertical edge, called *button bands*; one button band has buttonholes on it, and the other has buttons sewn to it. Button bands can be worked in various stitch patterns but they are commonly worked in ribbing, seed stitch, or garter stitch, to lie flat. Using needles that are one or two sizes smaller than the needles used for the garment give a neat appearance. For button bands, knit the band that holds the buttons first; mark the placement of the buttons on the band with stitch markers, and then, when you knit the buttonhole band, work the buttonholes to correlate with your markings.

Neckband
Button band

PLACKETS

Plackets are button bands that can be placed vertically at the neck in either the front or back of a sweater, or they can be worked horizontally in place of a shoulder seam. Pullovers for babies and toddlers frequently use the latter version. You should work the plackets in the same manner as the button bands above.

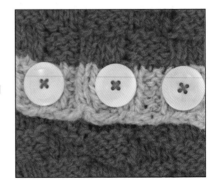

SEWN-ON COLLARS

One easy way to make a collar is to knit it as a separate piece and then sew it on. To determine how long to make the collar, you measure your sweater's neck circumference. When you have finished knitting it, you sew it on with the right side facing if it will fold down, so that you don't see the seam along the neck edge.

TURTLENECK AND MOCK TURTLENECK COLLARS

For a mock turtleneck like the one shown, you pick up stitches from the right side and knit in the desired pattern to the desired length. You can make it a crewneck by working fewer rows, or a long turtleneck that folds over by working more rows. You can knit the collar back and forth in rows by working it when only one shoulder seam has been sewn, and then sewing the collar's side seam later. You can also work this type of collar in the round after both shoulder seams have been sewn.

KNIT-ON COLLARS

You can pick up stitches along the neck to create a collar. When knitting a split-front collar directly onto a sweater, you need to be sure to pick up stitches from the wrong side if the collar is going to fold down.

Different projects and styles of sweaters call for different types of buttonholes. The size and type of button that you're using also influences your choice of buttonhole. However, the eyelet buttonhole, the 1-row horizontal buttonhole, and the 2-row horizontal buttonhole should get you through most situations.

HOW TO MAKE A 1-STITCH EYELET BUTTONHOLE

1 To make this easy buttonhole, work to the point where you want the buttonhole to be, and then knit 2 together and yarn over. Continue the row as established.

2 On the next row, work the yarn over as you would a regular stitch.

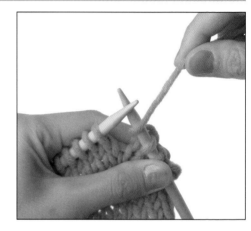

You have now made a 1-stitch eyelet buttonhole.

Note: You place buttons on the left band for women and on the right band for men.

HOW TO MAKE A 2-STITCH EYELET BUTTONHOLE

① Work to the point where you want the buttonhole, and then knit 2 together, yarn over twice, and slip, slip, knit; work the remainder of the row as previously established.

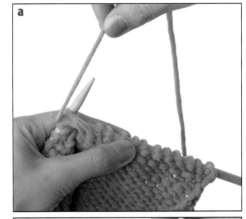

② On the next row, work across until you get to the yarn-overs. Purl into the first yarn-over (a), and then purl into the back of the second yarn-over (b). Continue across the row as previously established.

CONTINUED ON NEXT PAGE

TIP

Buttonholes and Bulky Yarns

Stitches that are worked in bulky yarns are larger than those that are worked in fine yarns, and the same goes for buttonholes. Sometimes even the smallest buttonhole, the 1-stitch eyelet, comes out too big for your button in bulky yarn. Consider omitting buttonholes altogether with bulky yarns; you can probably fit your button through one of the big stitches. See p. 176 on reinforcing buttonholes, if you have already worked them and they are too big.

HOW TO MAKE A 1-ROW HORIZONTAL BUTTONHOLE

1 On the right side, work to the point where you want the buttonhole to begin. Bring the yarn to the front, slip the next stitch from the left needle as if to purl, and bring the yarn to the back. *Slip the next stitch from the left needle to the right, and pass the first slipped stitch over it and off the needle. Repeat from * three times, keeping the yarn at the back the whole time.

You have now bound off 4 stitches.

Note: *For a wider buttonhole, bind off more stitches; for a narrower buttonhole, bind off fewer stitches.*

2 Slip the last bound-off stitch back to the left needle.

3 Turn your work so that the wrong side is facing, and bring the yarn to the back.

4 Insert the right needle between the first and second stitches on the left needle, and wrap the yarn around the right needle as if to knit.

5 Bring the loop through to the front as if to knit, but instead of slipping the old stitch off the left needle, use the right needle to place the new loop onto the left needle.

You have now used the cable cast-on method to cast on 1 stitch.

6 Repeat steps 4–5, four more times, and then turn the work back so that the right side is facing.

You have now cast on 5 stitches.

7 Bring the yarn to the back and slip the first stitch from the left needle to the right needle; pass the additional cast-on stitch over the slipped stitch to close the buttonhole. Work to the end of the row as usual.

CONTINUED ON NEXT PAGE

TIP

Centering Buttonholes on a Button Band

If you work the buttonhole right at the center of the buttonhole band, and sew the button right at the center of the button band, you will find that, when buttoned, you can see a strip of button band peeking out from under the buttonhole band. To ensure that the bands are properly lined up, and the buttons look centered, try working your eyelet or horizontal buttonhole 1 or 2 rows before you get to the center of the band. (How many rows you will work depends on your row gauge.)

HOW TO MAKE A 2-ROW HORIZONTAL BUTTONHOLE

1 On the right side, work to the point where you want the buttonhole to be placed, and then knit 2.

2 Insert the left needle from front to back into the first stitch of the pair that you just knit; then pull it over the second stitch and off the right needle (to bind off).

3 Knit 1 and bring the stitch before it over and off the right needle.

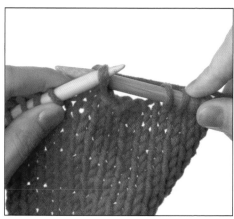

4. Repeat step 3, two more times.

    You have now bound off 4 stitches for the buttonhole.

    Note: For a wider buttonhole, bind off more stitches; for a narrower buttonhole, bind off fewer stitches.

5. Work to the end of the row as usual.

6. On the wrong side, work until you get to the bound-off stitches.

7. Make a loop with the working yarn as shown; insert the right needle into the loop and pull to tighten.

    You have now used the simple cast-on method to cast on 1 stitch.

8. Repeat step 7, three more times.

    You have now cast on 4 stitches.

9. Work to the end of the row as usual.

    You have now completed a 2-row horizontal buttonhole.

Some buttonholes need to be reinforced so that they don't stretch out and become distorted. Reinforcing a buttonhole also gives it a tidy appearance. The two methods covered here—overcasting and buttonhole stitch—should suit any instance.

HOW TO REINFORCE BUTTONHOLES BY OVERCASTING

1. Thread a tapestry needle with matching or contrast color yarn.

2. Bring the tapestry needle through from back to front, leaving a 6-inch tail at the back, and loop the yarn from front to back around the perimeter of the buttonhole, as shown.

3. End your stitching on the wrong side.

4. Weave in the loose ends.

HOW TO REINFORCE BUTTONHOLES WITH BUTTONHOLE STITCH

① Thread a tapestry needle with matching or contrast color yarn.

② Bring the tapestry needle through from back to front, leaving a 6-inch tail at the back.

③ Working from right to left, insert the tapestry needle from front to back, with the tip of the needle pointing toward the buttonhole, looping the yarn under the needle.

④ End your stitching on the wrong side. Cut the yarn, leaving a 6-inch tail.

⑤ Secure the ends at the back, and weave in.

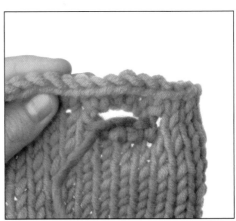

TIP

Buttonholes Too Big, or Too Loose?

Buttonhole stitch and overcasting can also work wonders on buttonholes that are too big. If your buttonholes are too big for your buttons, or will be after only a few unbuttonings, try reinforcing them using one of the methods on this page. If the buttonhole is much too big, or too loose, another option is to stitch it closed on each end to close it up slightly.

You can sew a zipper into the front of a cardigan instead of using buttons. Zippers are good for baby and toddler sweaters, as well as casual weekend cardigans and coats for adults. The following instructions are for sewing a zipper into a sweater, but you can use the same technique to attach a zipper to a knitted bag. Be sure that the edge that the zipper is sewn to is the same length as the zipper, or your garment will be distorted.

① With the zipper closed and the right side of your garment facing, pin the zipper along and under the front edges so that the edges are almost touching each other, and so that they cover the teeth of the zipper.

② Still working on the right side, use a contrast color thread to baste the zipper to the sweater edges to temporarily hold it in place. Make sure that your stitches are close to the zipper teeth for a firm hold.

③ Working on the wrong side, use thread in a matching color to neatly and evenly whipstitch the outside edges of the zipper to the fronts of the sweater.

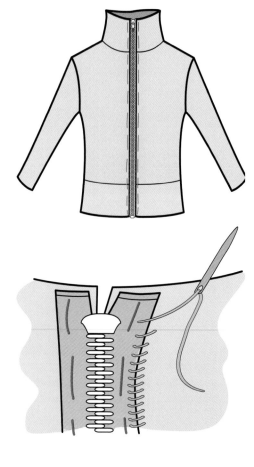

④ Turn back to the right side and neatly sew the edges of the sweater to the zipper, right next to the teeth, but not so close as to interfere with the zipper's functioning.

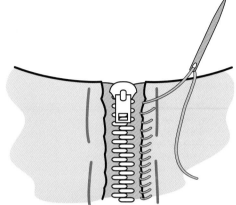

⑤ You can make a mini tassel, like the one shown here, or a tiny pom-pom to attach to the zipper pull, if desired.

TIP

More Zipper Tips

A straight, firm edge is best for zippers, and so if you are attaching to a ribbed or textured stitch band, similar to a button band, bind off knitwise instead of in pattern; this will leave a straighter, firmer edge. If you are attaching your zipper to side edges—edges that have not had the addition of a knitted band—consider using selvages (see p. 76) or working a row of single crochet along those edges to make them firmer and neater.

You can add a pocket to almost anything you knit—a sweater, a coat, a vest, or even a scarf. Patch pockets are the easiest to make. You just knit a square or rectangle to the size you want and sew it onto your knitting. You can also pick up the stitches from your knitting and knit the patch pocket directly on. Inset pockets, which have a less noticeable appearance than patch pockets, are a little more challenging, but if you know how to bind off, you can make those, too.

HOW TO ATTACH A PATCH POCKET

1. Pin the pocket in place exactly where you want it to be. Thread a tapestry needle as you would to sew your knitting together, leaving a 6-inch tail coming out one side of the eye.

2. Insert the tapestry needle from back to front, through both the knitting and the upper-right corner of the pocket. Loop the yarn around from front to back to front once more to reinforce the corner.

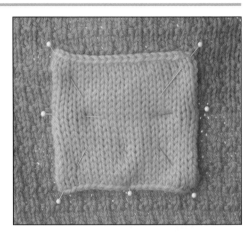

3. Sew on the pocket, using the overcast stitch that you used to reinforce buttonholes on p. 176, as shown, ending at the upper-left corner. Reinforce the corner as in step 2, ending with the needle on the wrong side.

4. Weave in the loose ends.

HOW TO PICK UP A PATCH POCKET

1. Using straight pins, mark the outline of where you want the patch pocket to be on your garment.

2. Weave the smaller knitting needle under and over horizontally along the stitches where the base of the pocket will be.

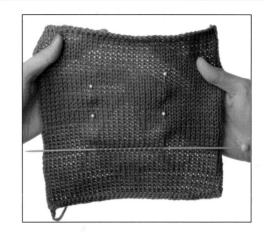

3. Using the yarn that you intend to knit the pocket with and the working knitting needle, purl across the picked-up stitches. (This first row is a wrong-side row.)

4. Beginning with a knit row, work from here in stockinette stitch (that is, knit across on the right side, and purl across on the wrong side) until the pocket is the length that you want it to be.

5. Bind off loosely.

6. Pin the pocket sides to the knitting. (See the photo of the pinned patch pocket on the previous page.)

7. Stitch the pocket sides in place, using the overcast stitch that you used to reinforce buttonholes on p. 176.

CONTINUED ON NEXT PAGE

HOW TO MAKE AN INSET POCKET

1. Knit the pocket lining or linings to the size indicated in your pattern's instructions. Instead of binding off the stitches, put them on a stitch holder. Steam the lining to block it. (See p. 146.)

   Note: Pocket linings are usually knit in stockinette stitch so that they lie flat. You can knit a pocket lining in the same color as the overall piece, or, if you prefer, you can knit the lining in an accent color.

2. On the piece of the garment that will hold the pocket (usually a cardigan front), work across the row on the right side to where the pocket will be placed. Bind off the same number of stitches as used to knit your pocket lining and work to the end of the row.

3. On the following row (wrong side), work across to the bound-off stitches. Hold your pocket lining so that the wrong side is facing you. (The right side of the lining should face the wrong side of the main garment piece.) Work across the lining stitches from the holder; then work across the remaining stitches of the main garment.

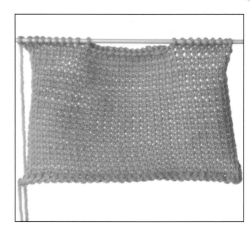

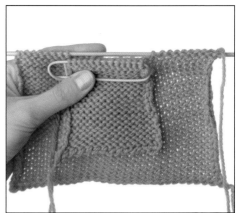

4 On the next row (right side), work across as usual.

5 Continue working this piece of the garment as established.

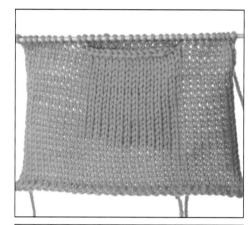

6 At the finishing stage of your garment, pin the bottom and sides of the pocket lining in place and stitch to attach them, using the overcast stitch that you used to reinforce buttonholes on p. 176.

7 Steam the sewn-in lining to flatten it, taking care not to press it, which would bring the outline of the lining to the front of your work.

Note: *You can also make an inset pocket by putting the stitches where the pocket is to be placed onto a holder after working across them on the right side. Then you continue across the row to the end and place the lining as shown here. At the finishing stage, you can then work from the held stitches to create an edging, such as ribbing, seed stitch, or garter stitch.*

A turned hem creates a tidy, crisp alternative to ribbing at a hemline, a neck, on a cuff, or along the button band of a cardigan. A turning row, or turning ridge, is worked at the fold line to make a neat edge that turns under easily. How the turning row is worked determines the look of the hemline.

HEM WITH PURLED TURNING ROW

To knit a hem with a purled turning row, knit the facing in stockinette stitch to the desired length, using smaller needles than required for the project. Then, purl the turning row on the right side. Work the garment from there using the needle recommended for the project. Finish the garment by folding over the hem at the purled row; pin and stitch it in place.

HEM WITH PICOT TURNING ROW

This pretty hem, which looks like a row of tiny scallops, works well on dresses and baby clothes. You work a picot hem similarly to a hem with a purled turning row, except that you work the picot turning row on an even number of stitches on the right side by working a knit 2 together, yarn-over eyelet pattern across, and ending with a single knit stitch. Finish the garment by folding the hem along the eyelet row, and pin and stitch it in place.

PICOT TURNED BUTTON BAND

When working a button band with a picot hem, you work the buttonholes symmetrically on either side of the turning row. Finish the band in the same manner as you would a hem, except that you reinforce the buttonholes (see p. 176) through the two thicknesses.

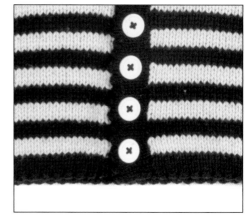

chapter 13

Decorative Details

You can liven up a knitting project by adding decorative details. You can add a pompom to a hat, fringe to a scarf, or tassels to the corners of a cushion cover. Sometimes a little embroidered stitch running along the edge in an accent color is enough to transform a plain sweater into something really eye-catching. Turn to this chapter for the basics on finishing touches: fringe, pompoms, tassels, embroidery, and crochet trimmings. These embellishments are not hard to do, and another half-hour of finishing will be time well spent. Please note that some of the steps in this chapter contain knitting abbreviations that are commonly used in knitting patterns. For a full list of the abbreviations, see the Appendix.

Make Pompoms and Tassels

You may want to accent a scarf, hat, or sweater with one of these decorative additions. Tassels and pompoms are both made from bundles of cut yarn, but they each have a completely different effect. You can use the same yarn that you used to knit your project or a contrast color. Try using a combination of two or more colors at once for a colorful appearance.

HOW TO MAKE A POMPOM

1. Cut two pieces of cardboard into circles the size that you want your pompom to be. Cut a pie piece out of each circle and then cut a circle out of the center of each of the circles. The two pieces should be identical.

2. Hold the two cardboard pieces, one on top of the other, and wrap the yarn around them tightly and densely. Cut the yarn end.

   Note: *Use less yarn for a loose pompom, as shown, or a lot more yarn for a dense pompom.*

3. Insert the scissors between the two circles and under the yarn, as shown. Cut the yarn all the way around the outside of the cardboard circles.

4. Bring a 12-inch strand of yarn between the cardboard circles and around the center of the cut yarn. Tie it tightly in a square knot.

5. Remove the cardboard and trim the edges of the pompom to make it nice and round.

HOW TO MAKE A TASSEL

1. Cut a piece of cardboard into a rectangle the length that you want your tassel to be.

2. Wrap the yarn around the cardboard to the desired thickness.

3. Thread a tapestry needle with a 12-inch strand of the same yarn and insert the needle between the cardboard and the wrapped yarn. Tie the strand's ends in a knot at the top edge of the cardboard.

4. Cut the tassel free along the bottom edge of the cardboard.

5. Wrap a 10-inch strand of yarn around the tassel a few times, about ½ inch down from the tied end, and tie the ends tightly in a knot. Conceal the strand's ends by threading them through a tapestry needle, pulling the needle through the tassel top, and trimming.

6. Trim the tassels' ends to neaten them.

TIP

Tassel Forms

You don't have to use cardboard to make tassels. DVD cases, slim paperback books (like this one), and notepads all make excellent tassel forms, and you can use the short or long side, depending on the length of tassel that you want.

Add Fringe

Fringe works well on scarves, throws, sweater hems, and ponchos. Combining two or more different colors or yarn to make fringe can have a lovely effect, so experiment by holding various odds and ends together next to your project to see how they look. Fringe can use up a fair amount of yarn, so make sure that you have enough before you begin. To make fringe, you need—in addition to the yarn—a pair of scissors and a crochet hook.

1. Determine how long you want your final fringe to be. Then cut the yarn to double that length, plus an inch extra for the knot.

2. Hold the strands together, with the ends matched up, creating a loop at the top.

3. Hold your knitting with the right side facing you. Insert the crochet hook from back to front into the lower-left corner, just above the cast-on row.

4. Use the crochet hook to take hold of your loop of folded strands.

5. Use the crochet hook to pull the strands through from front to back.

⑥ Pull the loop from under the cast-on row, and insert the fringe ends down into the loop and tighten.

⑦ Repeat steps 2–6 across the base of your knitting to complete the fringe.

⑧ When you have finished attaching the fringe, trim it with scissors so that it is even.

TIP

Fringe Benefits

Fringe doesn't have to go in the usual, predictable places. You can attach fringe along the vertical fronts of cardigans or knit jackets. A short row of fringe at the cuff of a baby sweater or women's jacket also adds a unique touch. Try adding fringe to the base of a rectangular knit bag, or around the perimeter of a knit cushion cover. The possibilities are limitless.

Make a Knitted Ball

A knitted ball is a fun accent to hats, scarves, shawls, and pillows. You can sew it directly onto your knitting, or first sew on a knitted cord (see p. 195) and then attach it so that it dangles. To make a knitted ball, you need a set of double-pointed needles several sizes smaller than your yarn recommends.

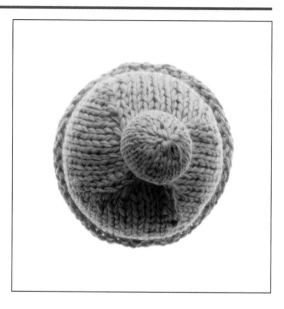

1. CO 8 sts, and divide among 3 dpns, leaving a 6-inch tail.

2. Join round, and using a fourth dpn, knit into the front and then the back of every stitch—16 sts.

3. K3 rounds.

4. Next round: K1, m1, *k2, m1; rep from * to last stitch, k1—24 sts.

5. Knit every round without further shaping until the ball measures 2 inches from the cast-on edge.

6. Next round: *K2tog; rep from * to the end—12 sts.

7. Rep last round once more—6 sts.

8. Cut yarn, leaving a 6-inch tail. Pull the tail through the remaining stitches, cinch tight, and secure.

9. Stuff bits of polyester stuffing into the ball through the hole at the cast-on end until it is firm.

10. Thread the tail that is left from casting on through a tapestry needle, and weave it in and out along the cast-on edge. Cinch tight and secure. (You can use this end later to sew the ball to your knitted item.)

11. Weave in the end at the top, pulling it down through the center of the ball and trimming it to neaten up the top.

Make a Knitted Flower

Knitted and crocheted flowers adorn knitting projects by adding a delicate touch. This is just one of many ways to make a knitted flower. You can accent the center of the flower with a button, or create two or more flowers in different gauges and layer them for a more three-dimensional look. The thickness of your yarn will determine the size of the flower.

1. CO 3 sts.

2. Row 1: Knit into the front and back of the first stitch, k1, turn, sl 1, k2—4 sts.

3. Row 2: Knit into the front and back of the first stitch, knit to the end—5 sts.

4. Row 3: K.

5. Row 4: Knit into the front and back of the first stitch, k3, turn, sl 1, knit to the end—6 sts.

6. Row 5: BO 3 sts, knit to the end—3 sts.

7. Row 6: K.

8. Rep steps 2–7 (rows 1–6) three more times, to create three more petals.

9. Rep steps 2–6 (rows 1–5) for the fifth petal.

10. BO stitches.

11. Sew the bound-off edge to the cast-on edge to shape the flower. Weave the needle in and out around the center hole, and cinch tight to close the center of the flower.

12. Sew the center of the flower—adding a button or a layer of two buttons—to your knitting. You can also attach a large French knot (see p. 205) or a knitted ball (see the previous page) to the center.

Make Twisted and Knitted Cords

You can use twisted and knitted cords for all kinds of useful details, such as hat ties, bag handles, and mitten cords. Twisted cords are easy to make. You can also attach pompoms or tassels to the end of a twisted cord for an added effect on hat or sweater ties. Knitted cords also have all sorts of decorative uses. Try looping and configuring one into a heart or flower decoration for a hat, or use a row of knitted cords in place of fringe.

HOW TO MAKE A TWISTED CORD

1 Determine how long you want your twisted cord to be. Then cut a few strands of yarn three times that length. Knot the strands together at each end.

2 Insert a knitting needle at each knotted end and pull the strands taut. Twist one of the needles in a clockwise motion until the strands are tightly spun together.

Note: If your strands are longer than your arm span, anchor one knotted end on a coat hook, a doorknob, or other stationary object.

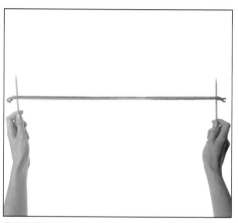

3 Maintain tight tension on the strands, and take care not to let them untwist; fold the strands in half—holding the fold loop firmly in one hand—so that the knotted ends line up with each other. Let go of the ends; the cord twists itself together, forming an elegant rope.

HOW TO KNIT A CORD

1 Cast on 5 or 6 stitches to one of your double-pointed needles.

2 Knit across the stitches but do not turn your work.

3 Push the stitches back to the other end of the double-pointed needle, so that you are ready to work a right-side row again. Insert the second double-pointed needle into the first stitch to knit as usual, firmly pull the working yarn from the end of the row, and knit.

4 Repeat steps 2–3 until the cord is the desired length. Bind off or cut the yarn and pull it through all of the stitches to tighten.

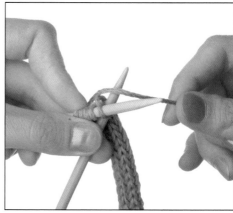

TIP

Easy Matching Buttons

Sometimes it's difficult to find buttons that suit your project. You can make your own buttons using yarn that matches or accents your knitting. Knitted cord knots and knitted balls all make excellent buttons, and they're not too difficult to make. To make knitted cord buttons, simply follow the steps above until your cord is about 4 inches long. Tie it in a single or double knot, and sew it onto your project. See p. 192 for instructions on how to make a knitted ball.

Fancy Knit Borders and Edgings

Sometimes a plain sweater or hat needs to be dressed up a little. You can work a fancy ruffle or border at the edge to add that accent to your knitting. The following ruffles, borders, and edgings are all easy to create. You can work them in the same color as your knitting or in an accent color.

BASIC RUFFLE

1. CO twice the number of sts that you want to end up with. (For example, if you are knitting a sweater back with 60 stitches, you CO 120 for the ruffle.)

2. Work in St st to the desired length of the ruffle, ending with a purl row.

3. K2tog across the entire row. You end up with half the number of st CO.

   Note: You can work 3 rows of g st to reinforce the decrease row.

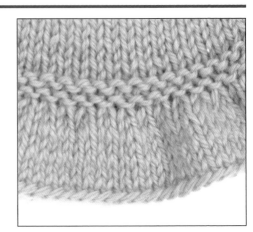

CURLY RUFFLE

1. CO a number that is a multiple of 2 sts plus 1, and that is 4 times the number of sts that you want to end up with, minus 3. (For example, if you want to end up with 60 sts, CO 237 sts for this ruffle.)

2. Row 1 (RS): K1, *k2, pass the first of these 2 sts over the second and off the needle; rep from * to the end of the row.

3. Row 2 (WS): P1, *p2tog; rep from * to the end of the row.

   Note: You can work the ruffle on smaller needles if you want it to be tighter.

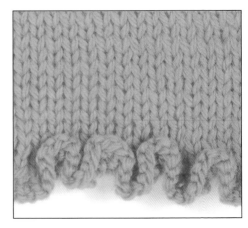

MINI SCALLOPS

1. CO a number of sts that is a multiple of 5 sts plus 2 (for example, 17, 22, 27, 32, and so on).

2. Row 1 (RS): K1, yo, *k5, [pass the second, third, fourth, and fifth sts over the first st and off], yo; rep from * to the last st, k1.

   You now have a multiple of 2 sts plus 3 on your needle.

3. Row 2 (WS): P1, *[p1, yo, k1 tbl] all in the next st, p1; rep from * to the end of the row.

   You now have a multiple of 4 sts plus 1 on your needle.

4. Row 3: K2, k1 tbl, *k3, k1tbl; rep from * to the last 2 sts, k2.

5. Rows 4–6: K.

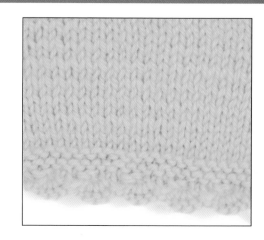

EASY POINTED BORDER

1. CO on 6 sts.

2. Row 1 (RS): K3, yo, k3—7 sts.

3. Rows 2, 4, 6, 8, and 10 (WS): K.

4. Row 3: K3, yo, k4—8 sts.

5. Row 5: K3, yo, k5—9 sts.

6. Row 7: K3, yo, k6—10 sts.

7. Row 9: K3, yo, k7—11 sts.

8. Row 11: K3, yo, k8—12 sts.

9. Row 12: BO 6 sts, k5—6 sts.

10. Rep rows 1–12 until the edging is the desired length. BO sts, and sew the edging to your knitting.

Knitting with Beads

Knitting beads directly into your work is an embellishment that can have varied effects. You can create elegant purses and evening wear by knitting delicate glass beads with fine yarns, or you can create a more casual look by knitting wooden beads into a thick, sturdy, natural-looking yarn. Because beading has grown in popularity, you can find a wide selection of beads at large craft stores. Be sure that your beads and yarn have compatible care instructions.

① Thread the end of the working yarn into a needle that is small enough to fit through the hole in the bead. Thread all of the beads that you will need onto the working yarn, sliding them down toward the yarn ball.

② Cast on stitches and work your knitting pattern's instructions.

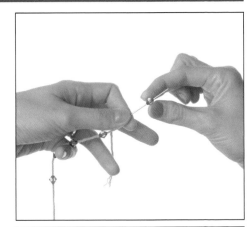

③ When you get to the point on a right-side row where you are ready to add a bead, bring the working yarn to the front, between your needles.

④ Slide the first bead up the yarn so that it rests snugly against the last knit stitch.

5 Use the tip of the right needle to slip the next stitch on the left needle knitwise to the right needle.

6 Bring the working yarn to the back, adjust the bead so that it is placed where you want it, and knit the next stitch snugly to hold the bead firmly in place.

You have now beaded 1 stitch.

TIP

Stringing Small Beads

Threading yarn through the holes of small beads can seem impossible, but you can use a beading needle and thin sewing thread to bring the yarn through the hole. Thread a beading needle with thin thread. Loop the thread around a fold in your yarn and then insert both ends of the thread into the eye of the needle. Slide the bead over the needle and then pull the needle, the thread, and the yarn through the bead hole.

Crochet Embellishment

You don't have to be a crochet expert to finish your knitting with simple crochet edgings or chains. A crochet edge can neaten and firm up an unstable or curling edge, and also add interest and color to a plain-looking project. In this section, you'll learn how to work a chain, which will enable you to add decorative cords, button loops, and picot trim to your crochet edgings. A picot edging makes a fancy trim that looks great on feminine sweaters and baby knits.

HOW TO CROCHET A CHAIN

1 Make a slipknot, leaving a 6-inch tail. Insert a crochet hook of an appropriate size for the yarn into the slipknot.

2 Wrap the working yarn around the crochet hook from back to front (creating a yarn-over loop) so that the hook catches the yarn.

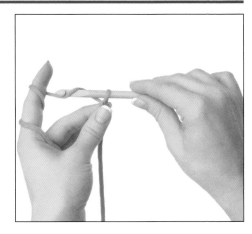

3 Holding the working yarn in your left hand and the hook in your right, pull the yarn-over loop on the hook through the slipknot.

You have now made 1 loop in a chain.

4 Repeat steps 2–3 until the chain is the desired length. Cut the yarn, leaving a 6-inch tail, and pull it snugly through the last loop to finish the chain.

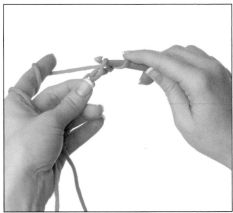

SLIP STITCH EDGING

1 Choose a crochet hook that is one or two sizes smaller than the needles that are used for your knitting. Insert the hook into your knitting at the right corner of the edge.

2 Loop the yarn around the hook (yo) and pull the loop through.

3 Insert the crochet hook into the next stitch of the knitting, yarn over again, and pull the loop through both the knitting and the loop on the hook from step 1.

You should now have 1 loop remaining on the hook.

4 Repeat step 3 across the edge. Cut the yarn and pull it snugly through the last loop to finish the edging.

Note: *If a crochet edge is causing your knitting to flare and stretch, try a smaller hook or try skipping a stitch every so often. If the edge is too tight, try a larger hook or try crocheting with a looser touch.*

CONTINUED ON NEXT PAGE

SINGLE CROCHET EDGING

1 Choose a crochet hook that is one or two sizes smaller than the needles that are used for your knitting. Insert the hook into your knitting at the right corner of the edge.

2 Loop the yarn around the hook (yo) and pull the loop through.

3 Working from the front, yarn over and pull a new loop through the first loop.

4 Insert the crochet hook into the next stitch to the left on the knitting, yarn over, and pull a new loop through.

You should now have 2 loops on the crochet hook.

5 Yarn over the crochet hook again, and pull this new loop through both loops that are already on the hook.

6 Repeat steps 4–5 across the edge. Cut the yarn and pull it through the last loop to finish the edging.

PICOT EDGING

1. Choose a crochet hook that is one or two sizes smaller than the needles that are used for your knitting. Insert the hook into your knitting at the right corner of the edge.

2. Work 1 single crochet (see steps 2–5 on the previous page).

3. Chain 3 (or 4, if desired).

4. Insert the crochet hook back into the same stitch, yarn over, and bring up a loop.

5. Yarn over again and pull the loop through both loops on the hook.

6. Single crochet 2 (into the next 2 stitches, moving left).

7. Repeat steps 2–5 across the edge to create picot edging. Cut the yarn and pull it snugly through the last loop to finish the edging.

Note: To create more space between picots, you can single crochet 3 or 4 times in step 5.

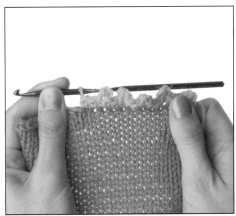

TIP

Make Your Picots Smaller or Larger

The scale of picot edging will change with the thickness of the yarn that you use to crochet it. You can adjust the size of the picots on your edging by working fewer or more chain stitches in step 3, above. For example, you may decide to make an exaggerated picot by chaining 5 or 6 stitches at that point. Alternatively, if you're working with bulky yarn, 2 or 3 chain stitches might be all that you need.

Embroider Your Knitting

Decorate your knitting with embroidery after blocking. An embroidered edging adds interest to casual knits, scarves, and throws. Embroidered motifs look best on garter or stockinette stitch. You can use yarn or embroidery floss to stitch on your knitting.

BLANKET STITCH

1. Thread a tapestry needle with your yarn. Tie a knot about 6 inches from the end. Pull the needle through at the edge of your knitting from back to front, until the knot stops it.

2. Moving right to left, insert the needle at the desired depth into the edge and bring it out to the front. The needle tip should overlap the yarn coming out of the starting point.

3. Repeat step 2 along the edge to create the blanket stitch.

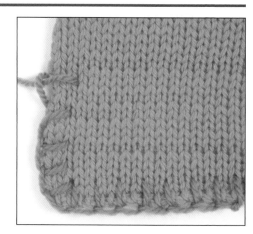

DUPLICATE STITCH

1. Thread a tapestry needle with your yarn. Pull the needle through the knitting just below the V that you want to duplicate, leaving a 6-inch tail.

2. Insert the needle under both loops of the V above the stitch to be duplicated; pull the yarn through.

3. Reinsert the needle into the hole below your stitch—the same hole that the needle came through in step 1—and bring it out again below the next stitch to be worked, all in one movement.

4. Repeat steps 2–3 for all duplicated stitches.

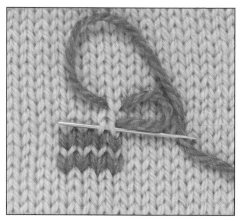

FRENCH KNOT

1 Thread a tapestry needle with your yarn. Tie a knot in the yarn 6 inches up from the end. Bring the needle through the knitting from back to front, pulling through until the knot stops it.

2 Grasp the yarn about 1 inch above the point where it came out, and wind it around the needle tip 3 times as shown.

3 Grasping the wound yarn, reinsert the needle right next to where it came out, and pull it through to the back to create the knot.

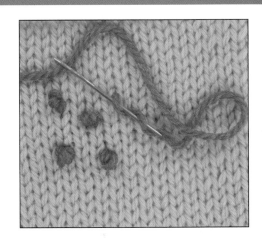

LAZY DAISY

1 Thread a tapestry needle. Bring the needle from back to front, pulling the yarn through, and leaving a 6-inch tail.

2 Hold the yarn in a loop and reinsert the needle right next to where it came out in step 1; bring the needle back out over the loop a petal-sized stitch away.

3 Insert the needle just below the end of the petal; bring it through to the front, above the stitch, ready to work the next petal.

4 Repeat steps 1–3 in a circle, until you have completed the daisy.

Appendix

Reference Materials

Refer to this Appendix for knitting abbreviations that are commonly used in knitting patterns, body and fit measurement charts, yarn yardage charts, knitting terms, and ideas for how to perfect the fit of your knits.

Knitting Abbreviations

Abbreviation	Meaning
alt	alternate
approx	approximately
BC	back cross
beg	beginning
bet	between
BO	bind off
C	cable; cross; contrast color
cab	cable
CB	cable back
CC	contrast color
CF	cable front
ch	chain; crochet hook
circ	circular
cm	centimeter(s)
cn	cable needle
CO	cast on
cont	continue(s); continuing
cr l	cross left
cr r	cross right
dbl	double (crochet)
dc	double cross
dec(s)	decrease(s); decreasing
diag	diagonal
diam	diameter
DK	double knitting
dpn(s)	double-pointed needle(s)

Abbreviation	Meaning
dtr	double treble (crochet)
epi	ends per inch
FC	front cross
foll	follow(s); following
g; gr	gram(s)
grp	group
g st	garter stitch
hdc	half double crochet
htr	half treble (crochet)
in(s)	inch(es)
inc(s)	increase(s); increasing
incl	including
k	knit
k1b	knit 1 into back of stitch
k2tog	knit 2 stitches together
k3tog	knit 3 stitches together
kfb; kf&b	knit into front and back of stitch
k tbl	knit through back of loop
kwise	knitwise
l	left
LC	left cross
LH	left-hand
lp(s)	loop(s)
LT	left twist
m1	make one
mb	make bobble

Abbreviation	Meaning
MC	main color
med	medium
mm	millimeter(s)
ms	make star
mult	multiple
no	number
opp	opposite
oz	ounce
p	purl
p1b	purl 1 into back of stitch
p2sso	pass 2 slipped stitches over
p2tog	purl 2 stitches together
p3tog	purl 3 stitches together
pat; patt	pattern
pfb	purl into front and back of stitch
pm	place marker
prev	previous
psso	pass slipped stitch over
p tbl	purl through back of loop
pu	pick up
pwise	purlwise
RC	right cross
rem	remain; remaining
rep(s)	repeat(s)

Abbreviation	Meaning
rev	reverse
rev St st	reverse stockinette stitch
RH	right-hand
rib	ribbing
rnd(s)	round(s)
RS	right side
RT	right twist
sc	single crochet
sel; selv	selvage
sk	skip
skp; skpo	slip 1, knit 1, pass slipped stitch over
sl	slip
sl st	slip(ped) stitch
sm	small
sp	space
ssk	slip, slip, knit
ssp	slip, slip, purl
st(s)	stitch(es)
St st	stockinette stitch
TB	twist back
tbl	through back of loop(s)
t-ch	turning chain
TF	twist front
tog	together
tr	treble (crochet)

CONTINUED ON NEXT PAGE

Knitting Abbreviations
(continued)

Abbreviation	Meaning
wpi	wraps per inch
WS	wrong side
wyib	with yarn in back
wyif	with yarn in front
yb; ybk	yarn at back
yd(s)	yard(s)
yf; yfwd	yarn forward
yo	yarn over
yo2	yarn over twice
yrn	yarn around needle

Abbreviation	Meaning
*	repeat starting point
**	same as *, but used to separate * instructions from the new instructions
( )	alternate measurements and/or instructions
[ ]	instructions that are to be worked as a group the specified number of times

Knitting Terms

The more you knit from patterns, the more familiar knitting language becomes. The following are explanations of terms and phrases that are commonly found in knitting instructions.

A

as established   Work in a particular pattern, as previously set.

as foll   Work as the instructions direct below.

at the same time   Work more than one set of instructions simultaneously.

as if to knit   Insert the needle into the stitch the same way that you would if you were knitting it.

as if to purl   Insert the needle into the stitch the same way that you would if you were purling it.

axis stitch   The center stitch between two increases or decreases.

B

bind off in patt   Work stitch pattern while binding off.

bind off loosely   Bind off without pulling the working yarn too tightly, so that an elastic finished edge is achieved.

block   Lay knit pieces out flat, and wet or steam them to the proper shape and measurements.

C

change to larger needles   Use the larger needles specified in the pattern, starting with the next row.

change to smaller needles   Use the smaller needles specified in the pattern, starting with the next row.

E

ending with a RS row   Work a right-side row as the last row that you work.

ending with a WS row   Work a wrong-side row as the last row that you work.

every other row   Work as instructed on alternate rows only.

CONTINUED ON NEXT PAGE

Knitting
Terms *(continued)*

F

fasten off   At the end of a bind-off, pull the yarn through the last stitch and tighten.

from beg   From the cast-on edge; usually used to direct where to start measuring a knitted piece.

J

join round   When knitting in the round, work the first stitch of the round so that the last stitch and the first stitch join, forming a circle.

K

knitwise   As if to knit; insert the needle into the stitch the same way that you would if you were knitting it.

L

lower edge   Cast-on edge.

M

marker   Something used to mark a point in a stitch pattern or to mark a point in your knitting, whether it is a plastic ring stitch marker, safety pin, or tied piece of yarn.

multiple   The number of stitches necessary to achieve one pattern repeat.

P

pick up and knit   A method of picking up stitches, as for a collar or button band, where the knitting needle is inserted into the work, yarn is wrapped around the needle as if to knit, and the new loop is pulled through.

place marker   Slip a stitch marker onto the knitting needle to indicate special instructions regarding the stitch following; or place some other sort of marker, such as a safety pin or strand of yarn, to indicate where buttons will be.

purlwise   As if to purl; insert the needle into the stitch the same way that you would if you were purling it.

R

reverse shaping When working something like a cardigan, where the fronts are mirror images of each other, instructions for shaping are given for one front; you need to reverse those instructions for shaping the other front.

right side (RS) The side of the knitting that will show.

S

selvage An extra stitch (or stitches) that will be used for the seam.

slip stitches to holder Put the stitches onto a stitch holder, usually to be worked later.

T

turning ridge A row of stitches, usually purled on the right side of stockinette stitch, where a hem will be folded under.

W

weave in ends When finishing a project, sew loose ends in and out of the backs of stitches or into seams to prevent them from unraveling.

with RS facing Work with the right side facing you; typically used when instructions are telling you to pick up stitches for a button band or collar.

with WS facing Work with the wrong side facing you.

work across Continue to work as established across the row of stitches or across a group of stitches on a holder.

work buttonholes opposite markers When working the fronts of a cardigan, place markers on the side where the buttons will be sewn and work buttonholes on the other front, opposite the markers.

work even Work without increasing or decreasing.

work to end Finish the row.

working needle The needle that is being used to knit or purl stitches.

working yarn The yarn that is being used to knit or purl stitches.

wrong side (WS) The side of the knitting that will not show.

Perfect the Fit

You can design handknits to fit any body type. Creating a perfectly fitting garment isn't as difficult as it might seem. It's mostly a matter of taking accurate measurements, determining ease, and calculating stitch counts based on the measurements. Here we look at how to perfect the fit of a sweater, which is probably the most demanding garment to design.

TAKING BODY MEASUREMENTS

To ensure a good fit, take detailed body measurements. Here's how:

1. Measure the **bust** or **chest** by placing the tape measure around the fullest part of the chest, at the underarm.

2. For the **waist**, measure around the smallest part of the torso.

3. For the **hip**, measure around the fullest part of the lower torso.

4. With the arm held straight at the side, measure for **sleeve** length from the edge of the shoulder to the wrist.

5. Measure from the underarm to the wrist to determine where to begin the **sleeve cap** shaping.

6. For a **short-sleeve** sweater, measure as for steps 4 and 5, only end at the point on the upper arm where you want the sleeve to fall.

7. Measure the circumference of the **upper arm.**

8. Measure the circumference of the **wrist.**

9. Measure the circumference of the **neck** (or the width of the back of the neck).

10. Measure the **armhole depth** from the top of the shoulder to the base of the underarm.

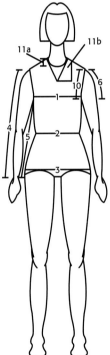
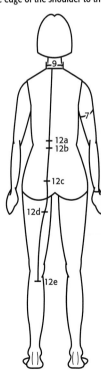

⑪ Also take some **neck shaping** measurements:

- For a rounded neck, measure from where the shoulder meets the neck to where the bottom of the rounded part should be.
- Do the same for a V neck.

⑫ Do not forget to measure the length along the **back** to best suit your sweater style:

- For a cropped, shrug-like sweater, measure above the waist.
- For a short sweater, measure at the waist.
- For a hip-length sweater, measure at the hip.
- For a fingertip-length jacket or tunic, measure at the thigh where the fingertips fall.
- For a long coat, measure anywhere from the knee down.

CALCULATING EASE

Some of your knitted measurements should be a few inches larger than the actual body measurements, or the garment will be too tight. The difference between body measurements and knit measurements is called *ease*.

When calculating ease, consider whether the sweater will be worn over a shirt or other clothing, and whether you want a tight or tailored fit or a more loose and boxy fit. Use the table below as a guideline.

What Size to Knit?					
Actual Body Measurement	*Finished Measurements*				
Chest	Tight Fit	Tailored Fit	Normal Fit	Loose Fit	Oversized Fit
31 in.–32 in.	30 in.	32 in.	34 in.	36 in.	37–38 in.
33 in.–34 in.	32 in.	34 in.	36 in.	38 in.	39–40 in.
35 in.–36 in.	34 in.	36 in.	38 in.	40 in.	41–42 in.
37 in.–38 in.	36 in.	38 in.	40 in.	42 in.	43–44 in.
39 in.–40 in.	38 in.	40 in.	42 in.	44 in.	45–46 in.

Measurement Charts

Included here are measurement charts for babies (sizes 3–24 months), children (sizes 2–16), women (sizes X-Small–5X), and men (sizes Small–XX-Large). This section also includes a head circumference measurement chart, which covers infants (preemies, babies, and toddlers), children, and adults. For more information about standard measurements, visit the Web site www.yarnstandards.com from the Craft Yarn Council of America.

Babies' Sizes					
Baby's Size (not age):	**3 months**	**6 months**	**12 months**	**18 months**	**24 months**
Chest					
Inches	16	17	18	19	20
Centimeters	40.5	43	45.5	48	50.5
Center Back Neck-to-Cuff					
Inches	10½	11½	12½	14	18
Centimeters	26.5	29	31.5	35.5	45.5
Back Waist Length					
Inches	6	7	7½	8	8½
Centimeters	15.5	17.5	19	20.5	21.5
Across Back (Shoulder-to-Shoulder)					
Inches	7¼	7¾	8¼	8½	8¾
Centimeters	18.5	19.5	21	21.5	22
Sleeve Length to Underarm					
Inches	6	6½	7½	8	8½
Centimeters	15.5	16.5	19	20.5	21.5

Women's Sizes			
Size	*X-Small*	*Small*	*Medium*
Bust			
Inches	28–30	32–34	36–38
Centimeters	71–76	81–86	91.5–96.5
Center Back Neck-to-Cuff			
Inches	27–27½	28–28½	29–29½
Centimeters	68.5–70	71–72.5	73.5–75
Back Waist Length			
Inches	16½	17	17¼
Centimeters	42	43	43.5
Across Back (Shoulder-to-Shoulder)			
Inches	14–14½	14½–15	16–16½
Centimeters	35.5–37	37–38	40.5–42
Sleeve Length to Underarm			
Inches	16½	17	17
Centimeters	42	43	43

CONTINUED ON NEXT PAGE

Measurement Charts *(continued)*

Women's Sizes *(continued)*					
Large	*IX*	*2X*	*3X*	*4X*	*5X*
Bust					
40–42	44–46	48–50	52–54	56–58	60–62
101.5–106.5	111.5–117	122–127	132–137	142–147	152–158
Center Back Neck-to-Cuff					
30–30½	31–31½	31½–32	32½–33	32½–33	33–33½
76–77.5	78.5–80	80–81.5	82.5–84	82.5–84	84–85
Back Waist Length					
17½	17¾	18	18	18½	18½
44.5	45	45.5	45.5	47	47
Across Back (Shoulder-to-Shoulder)					
17–17½	17½	18	18	18½	18½
43–44.5	44.5	44.5	45.5	47	47
Sleeve Length to Underarm					
17½	17½	18	18	18½	18½
44.5	44.5	45.5	45.5	47	47

Children's Sizes			
Size	**2**	**4**	**6**
Chest			
Inches	21	23	25
Centimeters	53	58.5	63.5
Center Back Neck-to-Cuff			
Inches	18	19½	20½
Centimeters	45.5	49.5	52
Back Waist Length			
Inches	8½	9½	10½
Centimeters	21.5	24	26.5
Across Back (Shoulder-to-Shoulder)			
Inches	9¼	9¾	10¼
Centimeters	23.5	25	26
Sleeve Length to Underarm			
Inches	8½	10½	11½
Centimeters	21.5	26.5	29

CONTINUED ON NEXT PAGE

Children's Sizes (continued)				
8	**10**	**12**	**14**	**16**
Chest				
26½	28	30	31½	32½
67	71	76	80	82.5
Center Back Neck-to-Cuff				
22	24	26	27	28
56	61	66	68.5	71
Back Waist Length				
12½	14	15	15½	16
31.5	35.5	38	39.5	40.5
Across Back (Shoulder-to-Shoulder)				
10¾	11¼	12	12¼	13
27	28.5	30.5	31	33
Sleeve Length to Underarm				
12½	13½	15	16	16½
31.5	34.5	38	40.5	42

Men's Sizes					
Size	*Small*	*Medium*	*Large*	*X-Large*	*XX-Large*
Chest					
Inches	34-36	38–40	42–44	46–48	50–52
Centimeters	86–91.5	96.5–101.5	106.5–111.5	116.5–122	127–132
Center Back Neck-to-Cuff					
Inches	32–32½	33–33½	34–34½	35–35½	36–36½
Centimeters	81–82.5	83.5–85	86.5–87.5	89–90	91.5–92.5
Back Hip Length					
Inches	25–25½	26½–26¾	27–27¼	27½–27¾	28–28¾
Centimeters	63.5–64.5	67.5–68	68.5–69	69.5–70.5	71–72.5
Cross Back (Shoulder-to-Shoulder)					
Inches	15½–16	16½–17	17½–18	18–18½	18½–19
Centimeters	39.5–40.5	42–43	44.5–45.5	45.5–47	47–48
Sleeve Length to Underarm					
Inches	18	18½	19½	20	20½
Centimeters	45.5	47	49.5	50.5	52

Head Circumference					
	Infant/Child				Adult
	Preemie	*Baby*	*Toddler*	*Child*	*Woman*	*Man*
Inches	12	14	16	18	20	22
Centimeters	30.5	35.5	40.5	45.5	50.5	56

Yarn Yardage Charts

You can use the charts on this page as general guides to estimate the yardage needed for various items.

Vest: Yarn Weights, Sizes, and Approximate Yardages

Yarn Weight	Baby/Child Finished Chest				Adult Finished Chest			
	24 in.	28 in.	32 in.	36 in.	40 in.	44 in.	48 in.	52 in.
Bulky	200 yd.	300 yd.	400 yd.	500 yd.	600 yd.	700 yd.	800 yd.	900 yd.
Worsted	250 yd.	350 yd.	500 yd.	600 yd.	700 yd.	800 yd.	900 yd.	1,000 yd.
Sport	300 yd.	450 yd.	600 yd.	750 yd.	850 yd.	950 yd.	1,050 yd.	1,150 yd.
Fingering	450 yd.	600 yd.	750 yd.	950 yd.	1,100 yd.	1,250 yd.	1,450 yd.	1,650 yd.

Pullover/Cardigan: Yarn Weights, Sizes, and Approximate Yardages

Yarn Weight	Baby/Child Finished Chest				Adult Finished Chest			
	24 in.	28 in.	32 in.	36 in.	40 in.	44 in.	48 in.	52 in.
Bulky	375 yd.	525 yd.	725 yd.	925 yd.	1,100 yd.	1,300 yd.	1,500 yd.	1,750 yd.
Worsted	500 yd.	700 yd.	1,000 yd.	1,250 yd.	1,400 yd.	1,600 yd.	1,800 yd.	2,000 yd.
Sport	600 yd.	800 yd.	1,100 yd.	1,400 yd.	1,650 yd.	1,900 yd.	2,100 yd.	2,300 yd.
Fingering	750 yd.	1,100 yd.	1,500 yd.	1,750 yd.	2,150 yd.	2,500 yd.	2,750 yd.	3,000 yd.

Hat: Yarn Weights, Sizes, and Approximate Yardages

Finished Circumference

Yarn Weight	14 in.	16 in.	18 in.	20 in.	22 in.
Bulky	60 yd.	85 yd.	100 yd.	125 yd.	150 yd.
Worsted	75 yd.	125 yd.	175 yd.	225 yd.	250 yd.
Sport	125 yd.	175 yd.	225 yd.	250 yd.	275 yd.
Fingering	150 yd.	200 yd.	250 yd.	300 yd.	325 yd.

Socks: Yarn Weights, Sizes, and Approximate Yardages

Foot Length

Yarn Weight	4 in.	5 in.	6½ in.	8 in.	9½ in.	10½ in.	11½ in.
Bulky	85 yd.	100 yd.	125 yd.	150 yd.	175 yd.	225 yd.	250 yd.
Worsted	125 yd.	175 yd.	225 yd.	250 yd.	300 yd.	350 yd.	400 yd.
Sport	125 yd.	175 yd.	225 yd.	275 yd.	325 yd.	375 yd.	450 yd.
Fingering	150 yd.	200 yd.	250 yd.	325 yd.	400 yd.	475 yd.	550 yd.

Numerics

A

B

C

Perfectly portable!

With handy, compact *VISUAL*™ *Quick Tips* books,
you're in the know wherever you go.

978-0-470-04578-7

978-0-470-07782-5

978-0-470-09741-0

All *VISUAL*™ *Quick Tips* books pack a lot of info into a compact 5 x 7^1/$_8$"
guide you can toss into your tote bag or brief case for ready reference.

Look for these and other *VISUAL*™ *Quick Tips* books wherever books are sold.

Read Less-Learn More®

Visual®
An Imprint of ⊕WILEY